The **Breast Cancer** Update

Alvin and Virginia Silverstein and Laura Silverstein Nunn

Titles in the DISEASE UPDATE series:

DISEASE
UPDATE

The **Breast Cancer** Update

Alvin and Virginia Silverstein and Laura Silverstein Nunn

Enslow Publishers, Inc.
40 Industrial Road
Box 398
Berkeley Heights, NJ 07922
USA

http://www.enslow.com

Library of Congress Cataloging-in-Publication Data

Silverstein, Alvin.
    The breast cancer update / Alvin and Virginia Silverstein and
Laura Silverstein Nunn.
        p. cm. — (Disease update)
        Includes bibliographical references and index.
        ISBN-13: 978-0-7660-2747-3
        ISBN-10: 0-7660-2747-3
        1. Breast—Cancer—Juvenile literature. I. Silverstein, Virginia B. II. Nunn,
Laura Silverstein. III. Title.
RC280.B8S4974 2007
616.99'449—dc22

                               2006032821

Printed in the United States of America

10 9 8 7 6 5 4 3 2 1

To Our Readers: We have done our best to make sure all Internet Addresses in this book were active and appropriate when we went to press. However, the author and the publisher have no control over and assume no liability for the material available on those Internet sites or on other Web sites they may link to. Any comments or suggestions can be sent by e-mail to comments@enslow.com or to the address on the back cover.

Contents

Breast Cancer

What is it?

An illness caused by uncontrollable growth of abnormal breast tissue cells that can spread to other parts of the body.

Who gets it?

Both men and women can get breast cancer, but more than 99 percent of the cases occur in women. Most of them are found in women over the age of forty.

How do you get it?

In most cases, the exact cause is unknown. In 5 to 10 percent of cases, it appears to run in the family. People who are overweight or physically inactive appear to have a higher risk of developing breast cancer. Drinking alcohol also increases the risk.

What are the symptoms?

The main symptom is a lump in the breast. At first it may be too tiny to see or feel, but it can be detected by a special X-ray called a mammogram. Later on it can be felt by touch as a lump or hardening. Sometimes there may also be a rash or a dimpling of the skin on the breast. Fluid may leak out of the breast.

How is it treated?

Usually by surgery. The cancerous lump or the entire breast may be removed. Sometimes the underarm lymph nodes are also removed. Treatment with drugs, radiation, or hormones may be used.

How can it be prevented?

A healthy lifestyle can help reduce the risk of developing breast cancer: Exercise regularly, eat a healthy diet and keep a normal weight, don't smoke, don't drink alcohol, and try to reduce stress. Drugs such as tamoxifen may be given to women at high risk to prevent the development of breast cancer.

Melissa Etheridge's first public performance after her diagnosis of breast cancer was at the Grammy Awards in February 2005.

1

Cells Gone Wild

ON FEBRUARY 13, 2005, rock-and-roll singer Melissa Etheridge wowed the audience as she sang a show-stopping version of legendary singer Janis Joplin's song "Piece of My Heart." It wasn't the first time that Melissa had brought her fans to their feet, singing and clapping. But this was the first time she had sung in public since she'd announced that she had breast cancer.

At first, people were surprised to see Melissa walk onstage completely bald. Melissa didn't look sick, though—she was jumping around the stage, swinging her guitar and singing her heart out. This was not just an ordinary performance. This performance gave inspiration and hope to breast cancer survivors everywhere.

Just five months earlier, on October 1, 2004, forty-three-year-old Melissa Etheridge was shocked to find a lump in her left breast while she was taking a shower. It was a very large lump. She didn't know why she hadn't noticed it before. Not only could she feel it, but she could see it. It seemed strange how suddenly it appeared. She had just had a physical that included a breast exam two months before. She had been very good about checkups and self-exams because there was a history of cancer in her family. Her grandmother and aunt had both died of breast cancer, and her father had died of liver cancer.

Even though she was on tour, Melissa knew she had to get her lump checked out as soon as possible. She did one more performance in Ottawa and then flew back home to Los Angeles. When Melissa got home—just two days after her discovery—she noticed that the lump looked even bigger. She went to see her doctor, who scheduled a biopsy right away. (A biopsy is a procedure used to remove a small amount of body tissue to check for cancer cells.) The day after her biopsy, Melissa was told that she had breast cancer.

Melissa canceled her tour and scheduled surgery so that the doctors could find out how serious the cancer was. During surgery they found a 4-centimeter (1.6-inch) tumor. They removed it. They also found that the cancer had spread to one of her lymph nodes. (Lymph nodes are masses of tissue containing white blood cells that help fight infections in the body.) They took that out, too. They also removed fourteen other lymph nodes, just to be safe: Breast cancer can spread into the lymph nodes and then through the blood-stream to other parts of the body. Later Melissa was told that she had Stage II breast cancer, which meant that it was in a fairly early stage. She was lucky.

Even though the doctors removed all of Melissa's cancer, the battle was far from over. She had to start chemotherapy ("chemo") and radiation therapy, typical treatments for cancer. She decided to shave her head even before she started chemo, since she knew the treatment would cause her hair to fall out anyway. Like other cancer patients, Melissa had a rough time dealing with the treatment. Some days it was a struggle just to get out of bed. Every part of her body ached. It hurt whenever she moved. She is very grateful to her family, who gave her the strength to get through it.

When Melissa was asked to sing at the Grammy Awards, she wasn't sure if she could do it. As soon as her chemotherapy treatments were over, however, she started to feel better. She was afraid that people might laugh at her bald appearance, but that didn't happen at all. In fact, it turned out to be an experience no one would soon forget.[1]

Now a breast cancer survivor, Melissa has changed her eating habits to live a healthier lifestyle. Being on the road, she used to eat a lot of fast food. These days, she eats more salads and chicken. She also tries really hard to cut down on stress, which she admits has always been a big part of her life. Melissa now feels great and hopes to keep it that way. She is just as busy as ever. In addition to her career, she is involved in a number of efforts to raise breast cancer awareness. Melissa is also giving the money earned from her song "I Run for Life" to breast cancer charities. The lyrics of this song have become a message of hope for breast cancer survivors: "I run for hope/I run to feel/I run for the truth/For all that is real/I run for your mother, your sister, your wife/I run for you and me, my friend . . . / I run for life."[2]

You have breast cancer is probably one of the scariest things a woman can hear. After hearing the diagnosis, many cancer patients start thinking about how much

Famous People Who Have Had Breast Cancer

Name	Occupation
Anastacia	Singer
Ingrid Bergman	Actress
Shirley Temple Black	Former child star actress and former U.S. ambassador
Sheryl Crow	Singer
Bette Davis	Actress
Melissa Etheridge	Singer
Edie Falco	Actress
Peggy Fleming	Olympic champion figure skater
Betty Ford	Former First Lady
Kate Jackson	Actress
Patti LaBelle	Singer
Kylie Minogue	Singer
Olivia Newton-John	Singer and actress
Sandra Day O'Connor	First female U.S. Supreme Court justice
Nancy Reagan	Former First Lady
Lynn Redgrave	Actress
Carly Simon	Singer
Jaclyn Smith	Actress
Suzanne Somers	Actress

time they will have left to live. Cancer sounds really scary, but it doesn't have to be an automatic death sentence. Research has come a long way since the mid-1900s, when cancer was considered "incurable" in most cases. These days, the chances of surviving breast cancer are good, thanks to early detection methods and better treatments.

2

Breast Cancer Through the Ages

WHEN GERALD FORD took the oath of office as the president of the United States in August 1974, his wife, Betty, stood next to him. She supported him, as she had done through much of his political career. A month later, however, Betty Ford found out that she had breast cancer. Now she was the one who would need the support of her husband and family.

Betty Ford was fifty-six years old when she got the diagnosis. Her doctors had found a small lump in her right breast during a routine examination. On September 27, Betty went to the hospital for a biopsy. President Ford stayed by her bed, joking with her to keep her spirits up. The next day, they were told that

Betty Ford, joined by her husband, President Gerald Ford, recovers from breast cancer surgery at Bethesda Naval Hospital. Mrs. Ford set a precedent for openly discussing her cancer and treatment.

the lump was malignant—that is, it was cancerous. Betty decided to have a radical mastectomy, in which the doctors would remove her right breast, some of the surrounding muscle, and the lymph nodes in her armpit. They found that two of the lymph nodes contained cancer cells, so she was treated with chemotherapy, powerful drugs used to kill any remaining cancer cells. The treatment turned out to be effective.

At the time, people did not usually talk openly about breast cancer. But Betty Ford was known for speaking her mind, especially on issues she cared about. She told the public that she had breast cancer and gave them details about her treatment. Betty wanted women to know that breast cancer was an important health issue. It was not something they should be embarrassed about. She encouraged women to examine their own breasts regularly and get mammograms, which can detect the disease early. As a result, Betty got a tremendous response from people all over the country. Tons of mail poured into the First Lady's office, the American Cancer Society was flooded with donations, and thousands of women made appointments for breast exams. Betty Ford may have saved the lives of thousands of women, thanks to her openness and honesty about breast cancer.[1]

These days, celebrities and other public figures are more willing to share their personal stories about breast cancer. People can also use the Internet to find information about the disease and learn where to get help.

An Age-Old Disease

Breast cancer is actually an age-old disease that has been devastating women for thousands of years. In the past, treatments were often cruel and the effects were often deadly.

The first descriptions of breast cancer were recorded as early as 1600 B.C. in ancient Egyptian writings. The author wrote about "the cold bulging tumour of the breast." At the time, the only available treatments were cutting out tumors with a knife (surgery) or burning them with red-hot irons (a technique called cautery).

Around 400 B.C., Greek physician Hippocrates described cases of breast cancer. He wrote that tumors in the breast are firm and continue to get harder. They do not contain pus, and they can spread to other parts of the body. These observations still hold true today. He also said that there was no treatment for hidden breast cancers, and that death was certain.

During the first century, Greek physician Leonides performed the first operation to remove the breast as a treatment for breast cancer. This operation is known as mastectomy. (*Mastos* is

> The first descriptions of breast cancer were recorded as early as 1600 B.C. in ancient Egyptian writings.

What's in a Name?

Hippocrates, an ancient Greek physician, coined the name for cancer. He called the group of diseases involving tumors, lumps, and bumps *karkinoma*, from *karkinos*, the Greek word for crab. Hippocrates thought the tumors looked somewhat like a crab, with their hard center and "legs" sticking out. (The "legs" are swollen blood vessels.) The Latin word for crab is *cancer*.

the Greek word for breast. The ending *-ectomy* means "cutting out.") Surgery was undoubtedly painful, since there were not yet any drugs to temporarily numb the body. In addition, doctors back then did not close up wounds by sewing stitches as they do now. Instead, they used cautery to stop the bleeding. They also did not have antiseptics, chemicals that kill disease-causing germs. As a result, the treatments often led to infection and death. Most surgeons at the time believed that it was better to leave the cancer alone.

Understanding Cancer

During the early 1400s, scientists began to learn more about how the human body really works. Studies of animals and autopsies (surgery performed after death) of humans provided a wealth of information. The invention of microscopes allowed scientists to discover cells, the basic building blocks of living things. Microscopes also allowed researchers to observe other body structures too small to see with the naked eye.

In the mid-1800s, German physician Johannes Müller reported that cancerous tumors were made up of living cells. These cells were abnormal, however, and looked different from normal cells. Müller also noticed that when cancer spread from the breast to other organs, the cells in the new tumors looked very much like those in the original breast tumor.

Surgery: On the Cutting Edge

In the mid-1700s, French surgeon Henri Le Dran had suggested that surgery could actually cure breast cancer if it was performed early enough, before the cancer had a chance to spread. However, without anesthesia or antiseptics, surgery was not an appealing treatment. In fact, many women chose not to treat their cancer if it

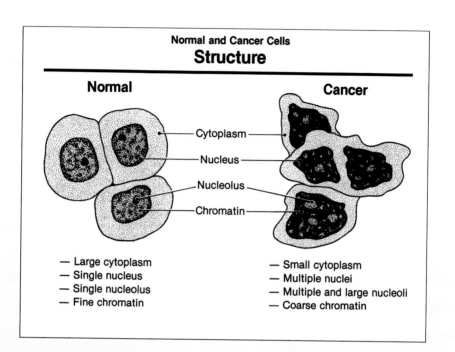

Normal and Cancer Cells
Structure

Normal	Cancer

Cytoplasm
Nucleus
Nucleolus
Chromatin

— Large cytoplasm
— Single nucleus
— Single nucleolus
— Fine chromatin

— Small cytoplasm
— Multiple nuclei
— Multiple and large nucleoli
— Coarse chromatin

What Is a Cell?

Your body is made up of trillions of tiny units called cells. Each one is too small to see without a microscope, and yet a cell can do many things. It can take in food materials, produce energy, and send out waste products. Many cells are specialized to do certain jobs for the body. Nerve cells carry messages to and from your brain. Muscle cells are working each time you walk or run, throw a ball, or turn the pages of a book. Skin cells form a covering that protects your body's insides. The specialized cells of your body work together to keep you alive and healthy.

would involve surgery. The tools used for mastectomies were guillotine-like instruments designed to remove the diseased breast quickly, in as little as two to three seconds. The wounds were large and took a very long time to heal.

In 1846, Boston dentist William Thomas Morton was the first to use ether as an anesthetic during surgery. In 1865 British surgeon Joseph Lister discovered that

In 1867, British surgeon Charles Moore introduced the first "standard" mastectomy.

carbolic acid was an effective antiseptic for killing germs. He started to clean wounds using a solution of carbolic acid. He eventually convinced other doctors to use the solution to wash their hands and to sterilize (make germ-free) surgical instruments and materials. With these discoveries, surgery started to become more popular. The procedure had become practically painless and relatively germ-free.

Even with the new techniques, however, the results of surgery were still not very good. Up to 20 percent of patients died as a result of infection. The rest of the patients generally did not live longer than two years after the surgery.[2] In 1867, British surgeon Charles Moore introduced the first "standard" mastectomy. He believed that methods of breast surgery that took out only part of the breast tissue might actually help to spread the cancer. Tumor cells that were left behind could travel to other parts of the body. Moore recommended removing the whole breast, as well as the lymph nodes in the nearby armpit and even chest muscles below the breast. Surgeons in other countries soon agreed and began to use this method. One of them, William Halsted, was a well-known American surgeon at Johns Hopkins University in Baltimore. In 1894, he published a report that helped to make the "radical mastectomy" popular. In fact, it was so popular that doctors began to call this surgical procedure the "Halsted mastectomy."

The radical mastectomy was criticized because removing the chest muscles not only left a huge scar but was often disabling. The procedure was so frightening that many patients would wait until the disease had become very serious to have it done. As a result, the Halsted operation did not really increase the survival

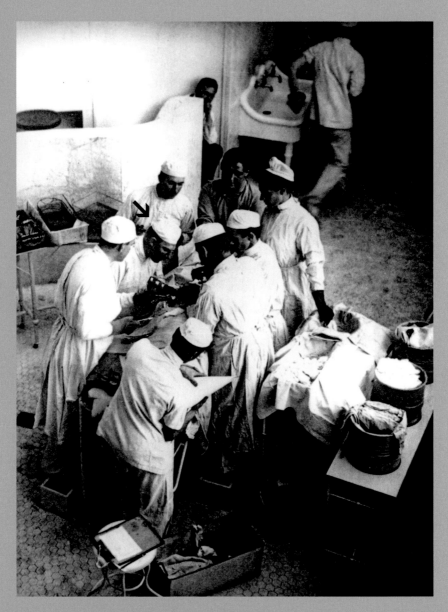

Dr. William Halsted performs surgery at Johns Hopkins Hospital in Baltimore in 1904.

rate—in many cases the cancer had already spread, and new tumors would soon appear. Nevertheless, radical mastectomy continued to be the "standard" treatment well into the second half of the twentieth century. (This is the operation Betty Ford chose to have in 1974.)

Discovering New Treatments

In the late 1890s, new discoveries led to other treatment options for breast cancer. In 1895, German physicist Wilhelm Conrad Roentgen discovered a kind of radiation that he called X-rays. Using a special "X-ray machine," he was able to make a picture of the structures inside the body. He made his first photograph of the bones inside his wife's hand. In January 1896, Emile Grubbe, a second-year medical student in Chicago, became the first person to use X-rays to treat a breast cancer patient. He got the idea after getting a radiation burn while experimenting with X-rays. The following year, Hermann Goeht treated two breast cancer patients with X-rays. All three patients had advanced cancer and died shortly after treatment. Researchers continued to study X-rays, trying to figure out safe doses of radiation.

In 1898, French chemists Marie Curie and her

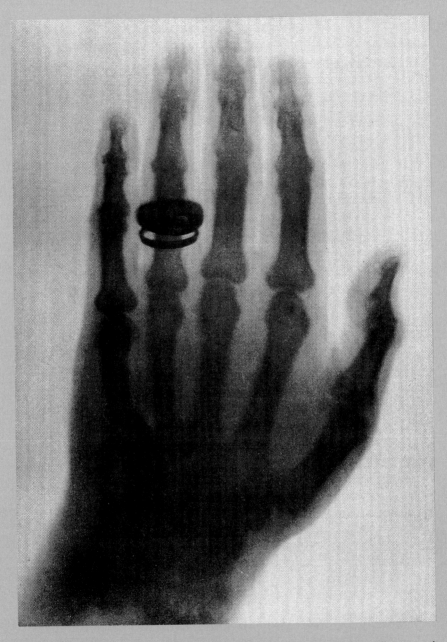

This is the first X-ray image ever taken. Wilhelm Conrad Roentgen discovered X-ray radiation in 1895 and took a picture of his wife's hand a week later. It shows not only the bones but also her wedding ring.

husband, Pierre, discovered radium. Radium is a radioactive element. Soon doctors started to use it to treat cancer. In 1906, British surgeon W. Sampson Handley suggested inserting a small tube filled with radon (a radioactive gas) inside the breast. The gas would destroy cancer cells that remained in the breast after a mastectomy. By the 1920s, radiation treatment had become widely accepted.

In 1922, English surgeon Geoffrey Keynes started to question Halsted's radical mastectomy. Keynes thought it was unnecessary and cruel. He suggested the removal of just the tumor along with a little bit of normal tissue around it. (This procedure was later called a lumpectomy.) He believed that this technique, combined with radiation therapy to kill any remaining cancer cells, would be enough. He treated many patients with early cancer, and found that over 70 percent of them survived at least five years.[3] Even though his results were encouraging, they were ignored by the medical community because the radical mastectomy was considered the "proper" treatment for breast cancer.

In the 1960s, long after Halsted's death, his theories and treatment were challenged once again. The radical mastectomy was based on the idea that a breast tumor

Good or Bad?

Radiation such as X-rays kills cells. In large enough doses it can cause serious damage to the body. When radiation was first being studied, scientists did not realize this. Marie and Pierre Curie, for example, handled radioactive elements frequently, without wearing protective gloves or aprons. After years of doing this, they both became ill. Marie Curie eventually died of leukemia, a cancer of the blood. Pierre probably had leukemia, too, but he was killed in a traffic accident before the disease could be diagnosed. Their daughter and son-in-law, who continued their work, also died of leukemia.

In small amounts, however, radiation can be very useful in medicine. It is used in the treatment of cancer. In addition, X-rays can help in diagnosing broken bones, tooth decay, and various diseases. (Marie Curie first suggested using X-rays for diagnoses during World War I, to locate bullets and shrapnel inside the bodies of wounded soldiers.) X-ray pictures of breast tissue, called mammograms, are used to detect tumors in the breast.

gradually spreads into the surrounding tissues. A breast cancer specialist at the University of Pittsburgh, Bernard Fisher, had different ideas. In experiments on animals, Fisher found that cells from a breast tumor spread through the nearby lymph nodes to other parts of the body, such as the brain or bones. The cancer cells settled down there and formed new tumors.

In 1971, a large-scale experiment involving more than 1,600 women was started. Some breast cancer patients received radical mastectomies, while others had a "total mastectomy"—removal of the breast and some lymph nodes, without the surrounding muscle. Early results, published in 1975, showed that women who had only a mastectomy did just as well as those who had a radical mastectomy—and they had fewer bad side effects.[4] The medical community responded quickly. Soon the radical mastectomy was rarely used. The new standard was the "modified radical mastectomy"—removal of the breast and lymph nodes in the armpit.

After the early findings, the Pittsburgh researchers ran a study comparing the modified radical mastectomy with lumpectomy. Lumpectomy was sometimes combined with radiation treatments to kill any stray cancer cells. The new experiments showed that lumpectomy with radiation was just as effective as the modified radical mastectomy in preventing the return of the cancer.[5]

Drug Treatments

During World War I, the Germans used chemical weapons called poison gases. Chemical weapons were not used in World War II, but both sides had stockpiles of poison gas—just in case. One of the ships carrying a type of poison gas called nitrogen mustard blew up. Sailors were accidentally exposed to the poison. Doctors found afterward that these sailors had unusually low numbers of white blood cells, disease-fighting cells that are formed in the bone marrow and lymph nodes. Researchers thought that if nitrogen mustard damaged these organs and stopped white blood cells from multiplying, it might help in fighting leukemia, a type of cancer in which abnormal white blood cells multiply wildly. Later, poisonous chemicals were also used to treat other kinds of cancers, including breast cancer. This approach was called chemotherapy.

3

What Is Breast Cancer?

IN MAY 2005, JENNIFER LYON thought she had faced the biggest challenge of her life—being a contestant on the reality show *Survivor: Palau.* It took a lot of strength and courage to make it to the final four, when she was finally booted out of the contest. Jenn's biggest real-life challenge actually came a few months later, when she was diagnosed with breast cancer. In meeting this challenge, Jenn found out what it meant to be a real survivor.

Jenn had first noticed something strange in the summer of 2004. She felt a string of several rocklike lumps in her right breast. She didn't go to the doctor to get it checked out because she didn't have any health insurance. Meanwhile, she searched the Internet to get information. The articles she read suggested that the lumps were probably scar tissue from the breast implants she had gotten six years before.

In July 2005, a year later, Jenn noticed another lump in the center of her breast and something hard in her right armpit. Now she knew something was wrong. She went to her doctor right away. First the doctor ruled out leakage from the breast implant. Then she told Jenn that she should have a mammogram, an ultrasound, and a biopsy. The tests came back positive. Jenn was diagnosed with invasive ductal breast cancer, which is classified as Stage III—advanced breast cancer.

Jenn was shocked. How could this happen? She was only thirty-three years old. She had always been a healthy person. She was very athletic. She had played sports throughout high school and college.

Survivor contestant Jennifer Lyon's biggest life challenge was her breast cancer diagnosis in 2005. Her surgeon removed both of her breasts and twenty-nine lymph nodes and was successful in stopping the spread of her cancer.

She had been a nutritional counselor and was good about eating fruits and vegetables. Her only real risk factor was that breast cancer ran in her family. Her dad's sister had died of breast cancer at an early age.

Jenn's family was very supportive. Her sister helped her go over all her treatment options. The first doctor she talked to told her that she should get chemotherapy immediately to shrink the tumors. Another doctor told her that she should have surgery right away because the chemo might not get rid of the tumor—or even worse, the cancer might spread to other parts of her body. Jenn decided to have a modified radical double mastectomy. Late in August, the surgeon removed both of her breasts and twenty-nine lymph nodes, eleven of which were cancerous. The surgery was successful. The cancer had not spread.

It took Jenn three weeks before she had the courage to look at herself in the mirror. It was quite a shock. However, she had already decided to have reconstructive surgery. In early October, she had new smaller breast implants put in. Jenn felt that these new implants really made her feel better about herself. Later in October, she started a six-month course of chemotherapy.

Afterward, she continued treatment with tamoxifen, a drug that will help to keep the cancer from coming back.[1,2]

Cancer of the Breast

Cancer is a group of more than a hundred diseases that have one basic thing in common: A change occurs in the body that causes cells to grow and multiply uncontrollably. The cancer cells choke out normal body cells and steal their food.

The type of cancer that develops is named after the part of the body where it started. Breast cancer is a kind of cancer that starts in the breast. As the disease gets worse, cancer cells can spread to other parts of the body, most commonly to the bones, liver, lungs, and brain. Even if the cancer has spread to the bones, it is still called breast cancer, not bone cancer.

> Cancer is a group of more than a hundred diseases that have one basic thing in common: A change occurs in the body that causes cells to grow and multiply uncontrollably. *Breast* cancer is a kind of cancer that starts in the breast.

You may think that only women get breast cancer, but both women and men have breast tissue. Men can get breast cancer, but it is not very common. In 2006, an estimated 276,000 women were diagnosed with breast cancer in the United States. Meanwhile, about 1,720 men were said to have breast cancer. An estimated 41,430 women and 460 men die from the disease each year.[3]

After skin cancer, breast cancer is the most common type of cancer that affects women. Usually it occurs in women over the age of forty, but, as with Jenn, the disease can also occur in younger women. The risk increases with age. A woman who lives to be ninety has a 1-in-8 chance of developing breast cancer during her lifetime.[4] For men, the lifetime risk of getting breast cancer is 1 in 1,000.[5]

Increasing Risk with Age[6]

A woman's chance of getting breast cancer increases greatly as she ages.

Age	Risk of Getting Breast Cancer
20	1 out of 1,985
30	1 out of 229
40	1 out of 68
50	1 out of 37
60	1 out of 26
70	1 out of 24

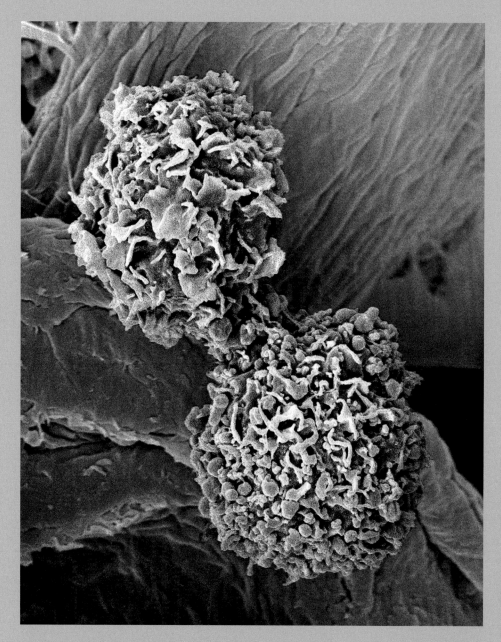

This microscopic image shows dividing breast cancer cells. Cancer cells keep dividing and push their way into healthy tissues, sometimes forming tumors.

When Cells Lose Control

Body cells normally grow and multiply. New cells are constantly forming in a growing child. Even in adults, new cells replace damaged or worn-out cells. Normal cells grow and reproduce in a very controlled way. They stop growing and dividing when they come in contact with other body cells. Cells also talk to each other by means of chemicals that travel through the blood or other body fluids.

Cancer cells do not act this way. Although they do not divide any faster than normal cells, contact with other cells does not make them stop multiplying. This happens because, at some point, the cancer cells mutated (changed) in various ways. They lost the ability to pick up and respond to signals that control cell division. They keep dividing and can't stop. They creep over other cells and push their way into healthy tissues. They may pile up to form masses called tumors. Since the tumor cells do not obey the normal contact signals, they may invade other tissues, damaging normal cells and stealing the nutrients they need. Soon they start to

Not all tumors are cancerous. Benign tumors are masses formed by cells that keep on dividing. These tumors are generally not life threatening.

choke out normal, healthy cells that have important jobs to do, such as making blood, digesting food, or controlling the movement of body parts.

Not all tumors are cancerous. Benign tumors are masses formed by cells that keep on dividing. They do not respond to the usual "stop" signals, but they do respond to contact with other cells. They may form huge tumor masses, but they do not invade other body tissues. If a benign tumor is removed, usually it will not form again. These tumors are generally not life threatening.

Malignant tumors are cancerous. Cells from these tumors may invade nearby tissues. They may also break away from the main tumor mass and travel through the bloodstream or lymphatic system to other parts of the body. There they may settle down to form new tumors. This spread of cancerous tumors is called metastasis. If a malignant tumor is removed, some of the cancerous cells may be left behind. Even a single cancerous cell remaining in the body can begin to multiply uncontrollably, and the cancer comes back. The damage that cancerous tumors cause to various important organs in the body can lead to serious illness and death.

About the Breast

Breasts are designed for one main purpose: to produce milk after a woman has a baby. Each breast contains lobules, tiny saclike glands that produce milk during breast-feeding. There are about a million lobules in each breast. A collection of lobules form a lobe. There are fifteen to twenty lobes in each breast. When milk is produced, it is carried through hollow tubes called ducts from the lobules to the nipple. The lobules and ducts are surrounded by fatty tissue, which gives them support.

The breasts need a plentiful supply of blood to provide fluids and nutrients for milk production. The blood flows through a network of blood vessels. The smallest are capillaries, tiny blood vessels with very thin walls. The thin walls allow an exchange of water, nutrients, and waste between the bloodstream and the cells. They also allow fluid to leak out of the bloodstream into the surrounding tissues. This fluid, called lymph, includes not only water but also various blood proteins, salts, fats, and other materials.

Lymph fluid leaks out of the blood vessels all the time. Sometimes it builds up in the tissues and causes swelling. Most of the time, however, lymph is returned

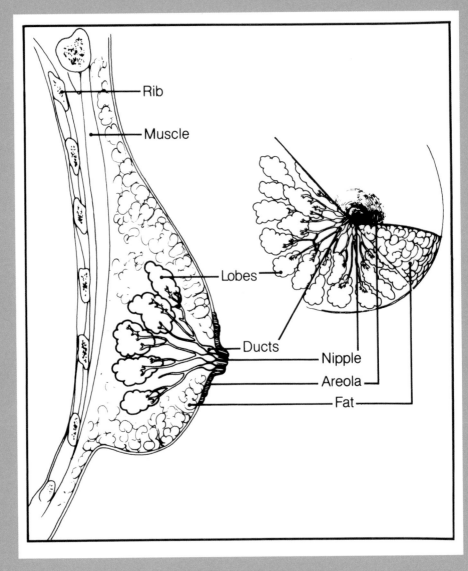

The anatomy of a breast.

to the blood by another network of tiny tubes—the vessels of the lymphatic system. Lymph vessels drain fluid from tissues all through the body and empty it into large veins in the chest, near the neck. The main job of the lymphatic system is thus to manage the body fluids and help keep blood circulating.

The lymphatic system also has another important job: helping to defend the body against germs and cancer. In addition to the lymph vessels, it includes lymph nodes. The lymph nodes are small bean-shaped structures where white blood cells gather. White blood cells are disease-fighting cells that help rid the body of infections. Lymph nodes are found in various parts of the body, including the armpits, neck, and groin. The lymph nodes in the armpits are called axillary nodes. The axillary nodes form a kind of chain from the underarm to the collarbone. Lymph from the breasts drains into the nodes in the armpits. When breast cancer is diagnosed, doctors usually biopsy these nodes to determine whether the cancer has spread to other parts of the body.

Chemicals called hormones affect the body in many important ways. They help to control chemical reactions in the cells. They also start and stop the growth and development of body parts and organs. The sex organs in both males and females produce sex hormones that act on other parts of the body. The ovaries of a female produce sex hormones called estrogen and progesterone. The testicles of a male make the sex hormone testosterone. It is estrogen that starts a girl's breasts growing during puberty. Estrogen and other sex hormones continue to act on the breasts for many years.

As a girl grows up, her breasts may go through changes in their shape, their size, and how they feel. Numerous milk-producing glands are formed during adolescence, so breasts often feel lumpy. (Normally, they

Hormones Make the Difference

If both males and females have breast tissue, then why do girls develop breasts and boys don't? The answer lies in their hormones. Boys and girls actually make the same sex hormones— testosterone and estrogen. Boys make large amounts of testosterone and very small amounts of estrogen. Girls, on the other hand, make large amounts of estrogen and very small amounts of testosterone. Estrogen triggers the breasts to grow, but testosterone stops the breasts from growing.

will not produce milk until they are triggered by hormones released at the end of a pregnancy.) Adolescent girls have more dense (thick), glandular tissue than fatty tissue. Meanwhile, the body produces several kinds of sex hormones, including estrogen and progesterone. The amount of each kind rises and falls in a regular cycle, lasting about a month. This monthly cycle is called the menstrual cycle. The varying amounts of hormones (including estrogen) that are released during the cycle can make the breasts feel different at different times of the month. For example, breasts may feel lumpy and tender right before the monthly period.

Women may also feel lumps in their breasts during pregnancy and breast-feeding. These lumps are usually harmless—the glands get larger when they are actively producing milk. As a woman gets older, her breasts become fattier and lose some glandular tissue.

Scientists have found that estrogen feeds breast cancer cells, helping them to grow and multiply. Therefore, they believe that the less exposure a woman has to estrogen during her lifetime, the lower her chances are of developing breast cancer. For example, the risk is increased the earlier she starts puberty and the later she starts menopause. (Menopause is the time during which a woman stops having her monthly period, and the ovaries no longer produce estrogen.) Earlier puberty and later menopause mean there are more menstrual cycles in a woman's lifetime. Thus, she has a longer exposure to estrogen. Hormone replacement therapy—taking sex hormones as medication after menopause—increases a woman's lifetime risk for breast cancer because of her longer exposure to estrogen.

Types of Breast Cancer

There are a number of different types of breast cancer. They can be put into two main categories: *noninvasive breast cancer* and *invasive breast cancer.*

Noninvasive cancer is also called carcinoma in situ. *In situ* means "in place"—the cancer has not spread beyond where it started. Noninvasive breast cancers are usually found in the ducts or lobules, and they have not spread to the surrounding tissues. Breast cancers in situ (especially those in the ducts) may later become invasive and spread to other parts of the body. But many women with noninvasive cancer in the lobules do not develop malignant tumors.

Invasive breast cancers

> Breast cancer can be put into two main categories: *noninvasive breast cancer* and *invasive breast cancer.*

start in the ducts and lobules and then invade the surrounding tissues. They may also spread to other parts of the body, including the bones, liver, lungs, and brain. There are various kinds of invasive breast cancers. The most common one is invasive ductal carcinoma, which accounts for about 80 percent of all breast cancer cases.[7] This type of cancer starts in the ducts of the breast. Cancer cells may then metastasize, or break away from the main tumor, and travel to the surrounding fatty tissue of the breast. The blood and lymph can carry these cancer cells to other parts of the body, where they may cause serious damage.

It's in the Genes

How does breast cancer develop in the first place? It can be traced back to a person's genes. That doesn't necessarily mean that the disease is inherited. It just means that something has caused a change or mutation in the genes that control cell growth and division. The mutation is passed from one cell to another through cell division.

Every cell contains genetic material, called DNA (deoxyribonucleic acid). This substance is a complex chemical made up of smaller units joined together in

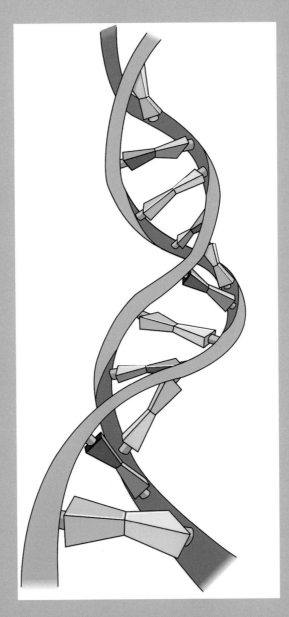

Every body cell contains DNA. It carries information for making new cells.
This illustration shows a model of part of a DNA molecule.

various combinations. Parts of the DNA form genes, which carry the instructions that determine the characteristics of a cell and blueprints for making new cells. The instructions are spelled out in DNA's chemical code.

When a cell divides, it splits into two daughter cells. These new cells are smaller versions of the original cell (the mother cell). Each daughter cell gets a complete copy of the DNA instructions its parent had. The daughter cells can then become mother cells to their own daughter cells, passing along the same genes they inherited from their mother, and the process continues. When the genes in a cell are damaged, the defective genes are then passed on to future generations of cells. Some damages to genes can change a normal cell into a cancer cell. Usually these changes affect genes that control growth and cell division. Researchers believe that it takes a number of damaged genes to turn a cell cancerous. Generally it takes years before enough damage builds up to cause cancer.

What Causes Breast Cancer?

Scientists are not sure exactly what causes breast cancer. Many people think that it is inherited. Indeed, researchers have identified a number of abnormal genes that are linked to breast cancer. These genes, however, are found in only 5 to 10 percent of all women with breast cancer.

Many inherited cases of breast cancer have been linked to two genes: BRCA1 and BRCA2 (*BRCA* stands for *b*reast *ca*ncer). Everybody is born with these genes. Normally, these genes help breast cells grow and protect them from becoming cancerous. People who inherit a mutated form of either BRCA1 or BRCA2 will have greatly increased chances for developing breast cancer or ovarian cancer. As many as 85 percent of women with a mutated BRCA gene will develop breast cancer, and up to 55 percent will get ovarian cancer. The average woman without the inherited mutated breast cancer gene has a 12 percent risk of developing breast cancer and 1.8 percent for ovarian cancer.[8]

Cases of inherited breast cancer are more likely to develop in women who have close family relatives with the disease, such as a mother or sister. The risk is also increased if a grandmother or aunt has had breast cancer. However, a family history of breast cancer does not guarantee that a person will develop the disease. Moreover, most women with breast cancer have had no

Ultraviolet rays found in sunlight, chemicals found in cigarettes, and radioactive materials are all carcinogens. They can cause cancer.

family members with the disease. Therefore, other influences must be involved.

Chemicals called carcinogens can cause changes in DNA that may lead to cancer. Studies have found that carcinogens in the environment—radiation and chemicals in things that people eat, drink, breathe, or come in contact with in their daily life—play a large role. Radiation, such as that given off by radioactive minerals, X-rays, and even the ultraviolet rays in sunlight,

Who's At Risk?

Even though the exact cause of breast cancer is not known, scientists have found that certain risk factors make it more likely for a person to develop the disease. Risk factors do not guarantee that a person will develop breast cancer—they just increase his or her chances. Here are some known risk factors for breast cancer:

- Being a woman: Breast cancer strikes mostly women.
- Getting older: Breast cancer is most common in women over forty.
- Having a close relative, such as a mother or sister, who has had breast cancer
- Starting puberty before twelve years old
- Starting menopause after age fifty-five
- Inheriting abnormal BRCA1 or BRCA2 genes
- Having two or more drinks of alcohol a day
- Being exposed to large amounts of radiation (such as X-rays or UV rays)
- Never being pregnant
- Having your first child after age thirty
- Smoking cigarettes and being exposed to secondhand smoke
- Becoming overweight as an adult (especially after menopause)
- Taking hormone replacement medication
- Poor diet that is low in fruits and vegetables

may damage genes and lead to cancer. Cancer-causing chemicals can be found in cigarettes, certain foods, and building materials.

A number of studies have shown that obesity (being extremely overweight) in adulthood, especially after menopause, may lead to cancer. Fat tissue produces estrogen. So even after the ovaries have stopped producing estrogen, obese women's bodies are still making the hormone. The continued exposure to the hormone increases their risk of developing breast cancer.

A diet that is low in fruits and vegetables could also lead to cancer. Many fruits and vegetables contain important chemicals that actually protect people from cancer.

It seems that there is no single cause for breast cancer. Usually a combination of factors is involved.

4

Diagnosis and Treatment

WHEN SHE WAS just thirteen years old, Dakoda Dowd was a star golfer. As a young child, she used to watch her dad play golf. When she was only four, she tried swinging a club herself. Her dad couldn't believe it when he saw her drive the ball high and far across the field. He knew then that she was a natural. Dakoda loved playing golf. She promised to work hard so that she could be a professional golfer someday. Her parents hired a golf coach and entered Dakoda in junior golf tournaments. All her dedication and hard work paid off, as she won over 185 trophies. But in 2002, Dakoda started to lose her focus on golf. She had a new focus in her life: Her mom was

Dakoda Dowd, left, her mother, Kelly Jo, and her father, Michael, celebrate Dakoda's win at the Ginn Open LPGA golf tournament in April 2006.

diagnosed with breast cancer. Suddenly, spending time with her mom seemed more important.

Dakoda's mom, Kelly Jo, was thirty-six years old when she got the diagnosis. She had first discovered a lump in her right breast in December 2001. Her doctor told her it was probably nothing to worry about, but that she should get a mammogram anyway. Kelly Jo was so busy that she put off getting the test for months. When she finally got around to it ten months later, her doctor diagnosed breast cancer. Kelly Jo decided to get a double mastectomy. Twenty lymph nodes were also removed; two of them were cancerous. Afterward, Kelly Jo had chemotherapy and radiation treatments, and dealt with the usual side effects: hair loss, weight loss, dry skin, and extreme tiredness and weakness. Dakoda, who shares a very close bond with her mom, was there for her every step of the way. Kelly Jo admitted that she really didn't think she could have fought the cancer, but her daughter gave her the strength to get through it.

Kelly Jo started to feel well again. She went back to work, and her hair grew back. Then in May 2005, she started to feel achy. She thought it was due to exercising. Near the end of the month, however, a bone scan revealed that her cancer had spread to her hip bone and her liver. She now had Stage IV cancer—the most advanced and least treatable kind. The doctors told her that she had six months to a year to live.

Kelly Jo did not think she had enough strength to go through more chemotherapy, but her daughter convinced her. She would do it for Dakoda. Meanwhile, even though spending time with her mom was her number one focus, Dakoda never stopped playing golf. Kelly Jo didn't want her to stop. Dakoda's dream was to have her mom live to see her play against pro golfers at the Ladies Professional Golf Association (LPGA) tournament in the Ginn Clubs & Resorts near Orlando, Florida, scheduled in April 2006. That would be nearly a year after Kelly Jo had been told she had up to a year to live.

Kelly Jo went through more chemotherapy, this time using different drugs that had less severe side effects. She was well enough to see her daughter play in the LPGA tournament. Kelly Jo was so proud. The mother-daughter team decided to talk to reporters about Kelly Jo's illness. They wanted to let people know how important it is to detect breast cancer early, before it's too late. She told them how she wished she hadn't waited so long to be tested after she felt her lump. Their new focus was to raise breast cancer awareness among the public and to help raise money for research.[1, 2]

Breast Self-Exams

When you have a cold, you may cough and sneeze and have a stuffy nose. You know that you are sick. With breast cancer, usually there are no obvious symptoms in its early stages. And yet, early detection is very important. Medical experts say the best way to catch

Medical experts say the best way to catch breast cancer early is to do regular breast self-exams, or BSEs.

breast cancer early is to do regular breast self-exams, or BSEs. This is a breast exam that a woman gives herself in her own home.

Women should start doing BSEs around twenty years old. That way they can become familiar with their breasts—how they look and how they feel. Then as they grow older, they will know when something doesn't look or feel right. Young women who have never done a

The Breast Self-Exam

1) HOW DO THE BREASTS LOOK?

Undress from the waist up and look at both breasts in the mirror. Does anything look unusual? Are there any changes in the nipples? Are there any dimples or changes in the skin? The breasts should be examined with the arms down along the sides, and then with the arms raised up.

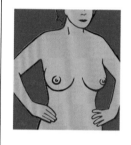

2) HOW DO THE BREASTS FEEL?

A shower is a convenient place to do this part of the BSE, as soapy hands can move over the breasts more easily. Examine the breasts one at a time. Raise one arm, with the hand behind your head. Use the other hand to feel the breast.

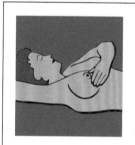

Think of the breast as a circle. Move the fingers in a spiral motion from the outside to the inside of the circle, gradually getting closer to the nipple. (Using mild to firm pressure can help to feel the deep layers of tissue.) Are there any unusual lumps that weren't there before? Is there something hard, like a marble, or a lump with a strange shape? Also check the sides of the breast and the armpit for lumps. Then do the same exam for the other breast and armpit.

BSE before might be surprised to find that their breasts feel a little lumpy, rather than smooth. As mentioned earlier, this lumpiness is actually breast tissue—and it is perfectly normal. A BSE should be done at least once a month, around the same time. A good time to do it is about a week after the monthly period starts. This is when the breasts are the least likely to be lumpy. They are also less likely to be swollen or tender. The illustration on page 57 shows how to do a BSE.

What if you do find a strange lump? Fortunately, most lumps—about 80 percent of them—are benign (not cancerous).[3] Benign breast lumps usually have smooth edges and move a little if they are pushed. For some women, the hormonal ups and downs during their menstrual cycle can cause changes in their breast tissue. These changes are known as fibrocystic breast changes. At least half of all women have these changes. They develop lumps in both breasts, which become tender and swollen right before their period. The lumps are actually milk ducts and surrounding tissues that grow and expand to form fluid-filled sacs called cysts. Fibrocystic changes are

> Fortunately, most lumps—about 80 percent of them—are not cancerous.

actually the most common cause of benign breast lumps among women between ages thirty-five and fifty.

Finding a strange lump in the breast can be scary for any woman. But when it comes to breast cancer, what she doesn't know *can* hurt her. It is important to get any unusual lump checked out by a doctor.

The doctor will first gather information about the patient's medical history, including any family history

Symptom Checklist

In its early stages, breast cancer may not cause pain or any symptoms at all. As the disease develops, however, there may be noticeable changes in the breast or underarm. Possible signs and symptoms of breast cancer may include the following:

- Lumps in the breast. They may be hard or soft, and their edges may be rounded or uneven.

- A lump in the underarm area.

- Swelling of part of the breast.

- Dimpling of the breast.

- Nipple pain or nipple turning inward.

- Redness or scaling of the nipple or breast skin.

- Fluid other than breast milk leaking out of the nipple.

Anyone who has some or all of these signs and symptoms should see a doctor.

Screening Tests

Medical experts believe that screening for breast cancer can save many lives. *Screening* means testing seemingly healthy people for a particular illness. Such screening tests include breast self-exams, clinical exams, and mammograms. The American Cancer Society recommends that women in their twenties and thirties have a clinical exam every three years. Women over forty should have a mammogram and clinical exam every year.

of breast cancer. Then the patient will be given a clinical exam, which is like a breast self-exam, but it is done by a doctor. The next step involves tests that can make an accurate diagnosis.

Diagnostic Tests

A mammogram is an effective tool for detecting breast cancer. This test is basically an X-ray of the breast. X-rays pass through soft tissue more easily than through dense (thick) tissue, such as bone. Bones show up on X-rays. Usually tumors are also rather dense and show up against the soft tissues around them.

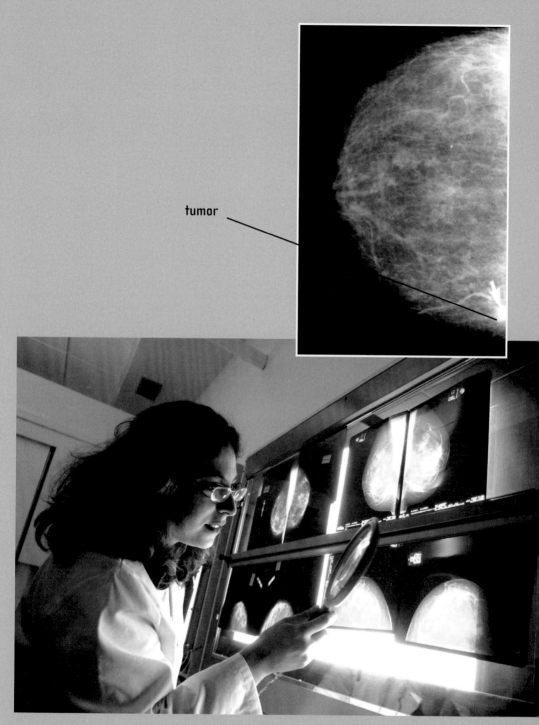

tumor

A radiologist examines X-ray images from a mammography.

A mammogram is an effective tool for detecting breast cancer. This test is basically an X-ray of the breast.

Like bones, these tumors will appear white on the X-ray film, and the neighboring tissues will appear darker. Some tumors, however, are not as dense as the surrounding tissue, or they may be very small, so they do not show up on the film. In addition, tumors may be missed in women with very dense breast tissue. Therefore, even though mammograms have been used to detect many cases of breast cancer, they are not foolproof.

Calcifications—small deposits of calcium—can also be an important clue to breast cancer. They are commonly seen in breast X-rays, and most are a normal finding. They look like grains of sand. Very tiny calcifications (microcalcifications), however, may be found in growing tumors. The radiologist (a doctor who analyzes X-ray images) will advise which calcifications may indicate a cancerous tumor and need to be studied further.

If the mammogram shows a suspicious lump or calcification, the doctor may order additional tests. One test may be an ultrasound. In an ultrasound, reflected sound waves are used to produce images of structures inside the human body. Sound waves are sent into the body and bounce off various structures inside, forming "echos." The way the sound waves bounce gives information about the size, shape, and density of the internal structures. A computer turns this information into a detailed image, called a sonogram. An ultrasound can determine whether the mass is a fluid-filled cyst or a solid tumor. (Patients who are under thirty years old are more likely to be given an ultrasound rather than a mammogram because they tend to have dense breast tissue.)

Another diagnostic test is the CT scan or CAT (computerized axial tomography) scan. This method uses tiny streams of X-rays sent through the body at various angles to produce pictures that are far clearer and more detailed than an ordinary X-ray image. The CT scan can detect tumors in such internal organs as the brain, lungs, and pancreas. It can provide valuable information about the tumor's exact location, size, and type. However, it cannot detect very small tumors, and it may not show where the cancer has spread.

An MRI (magnetic resonance imaging) scan uses a strong magnetic field and radio waves that pass through the body. It can produce clear images of almost any organ in the body. An MRI scan is more sophisticated

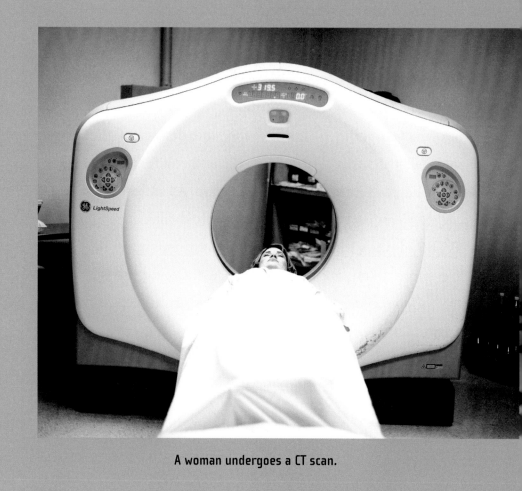

A woman undergoes a CT scan.

than a CT scan. It provides better pictures and is better able to identify certain tumors. However, it doesn't show calcifications as well as an ordinary X-ray or CT scan. An MRI can be helpful in identifying breast cancers in dense breasts, but it is not a replacement for mammograms.

Biopsy

If diagnostic testing shows a solid tumor, a biopsy is needed to determine whether the mass is benign or malignant. In a needle biopsy, a long hollow needle is used to remove fluid and a small tissue sample from the tumor or mass. A technician then examines the sample under a microscope and checks for cancer cells. Usually this procedure will show whether or not the tumor is cancerous. In some cases, however, the doctor may prefer to do a surgical biopsy if the tumor is harder to locate—for example, near the ribs or armpit. In a surgical biopsy, either the entire lump or part of it is removed, along with some surrounding tissues.

After a diagnosis is made, some tests may help to show whether the cancer has metastasized (spread to other parts of the body), and if it has, where. Chest X-rays are used to see whether the cancer has spread to the lungs. A blood test may be taken to see whether the cancer has spread to the liver. A bone scan may be used to see if the cancer has spread to the bones.

Certain tests may help the doctor understand more about the cancer, which can help in determining the treatment. For example, hormone receptor tests can show whether hormones (estrogen and progesterone)

Technicians examine tissue samples under a microscope to check for cancer cells.

are helping the cancer to grow. If the test is positive, then hormone therapy may work against the cancer. (Hormone therapy involves drugs that will starve the cancer of the key hormones.)

Staging Cancer

Diagnostic testing is used not just for detecting cancer, but also for staging the disease. "Staging" is a process that determines how serious the cancer is, where it is located, and how far it has spread. To stage solid tumors, the doctor examines the size of the tumor, the lymph nodes affected, and where the cancer has spread. Staging the cancer is very important to figure out the best treatment. A number of tests may be used for staging. These may include X-rays, MRIs, CT (or CAT) scans, and others mentioned earlier.

The TNM system is commonly used for staging cancers. It includes three important elements: *T* refers to the size of the *t*umor and whether it has invaded nearby tissues and organs. *N* describes whether the cancer has spread to nearby lymph *n*odes, and if so, how far it has spread along the lymphatic system. *M* indicates whether the cancer has spread to other organs in the body, forming new tumors (*m*etastasis), and if so, how many organs are involved.

Once the TNM values have been determined, they are combined into a more general classification to indicate the stage of the cancer. There are five stages, from 0 to IV. The higher the number, the more serious the condition. A Stage 0 cancer is a single tumor that is still small and has not spread to any lymph nodes or other organs.

LUMPECTOMY

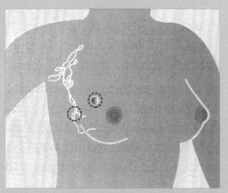

MODIFIED RADICAL MASTECTOMY

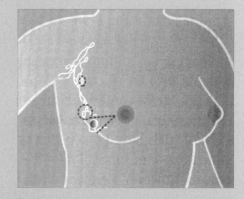

PARTIAL MASTECTOMY

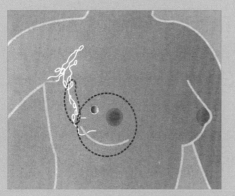

RADICAL MASTECTOMY

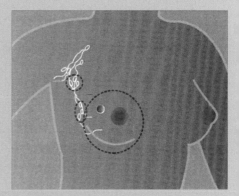

TOTAL MASTECTOMY

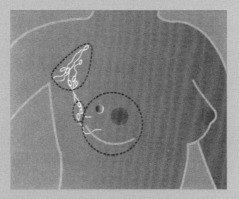

These drawings illustrate five surgical treatments for breast cancer. The areas within the dashed lines show the parts that are removed by the surgery.

How Is Breast Cancer Treated?

Surgery is one treatment option that works best when the cancer is discovered early. If a tumor is cut out before it has metastasized, the patient can be completely cured. The surgeon must try to get out all of the cancer cells. That means taking out some of the normal tissues that the cancer may have invaded, and possibly lymph nodes as well. If any cancer cells are left, they can begin to multiply again after the operation. Imagine this: A

> There are basically two types of surgery for breast cancer: lumpectomy and mastectomy. In a lumpectomy, the surgeon cuts out the tumor. In a mastectomy, the entire breast is removed.

tumor the size of your thumb contains *one billion* malignant cells. If an operation removed 99.9 percent of the tumor, there would still be one million cancer cells left.

There are basically two types of surgery for breast cancer: lumpectomy and mastectomy. In a lumpectomy, the surgeon cuts out the tumor and some normal breast tissue around it. Lymph nodes may also be removed from the armpit. In a mastectomy, the entire breast is removed. Rarely, some women need a double mastectomy—the removal of both breasts—to prevent cancer from developing in the other breast.

Getting a mastectomy can greatly affect how a woman feels about herself. Losing one or both breasts can be shocking and upsetting. Many women choose to have breast implants put in either during their surgery or at a later date. This helps to boost their self-esteem and confidence, which can help in the healing process.

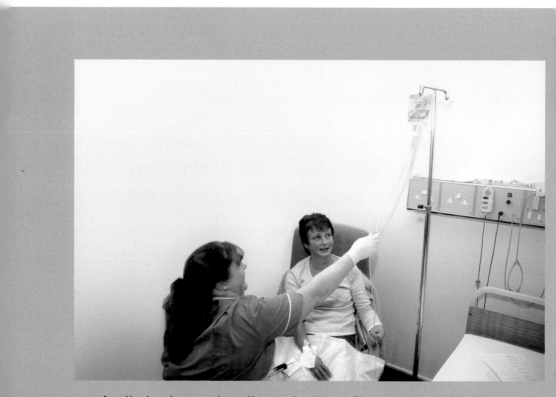

A patient undergoes chemotherapy treatment. The nurse is adjusting the amount of medicine coming out of the IV.

Often cancer treatment involves a combination of surgery followed by chemotherapy and radiation treatments in an effort to kill any remaining cancer cells.

Chemotherapy

Chemotherapy—treatment with chemicals—is the most effective approach in fighting cancer. The chemicals used are powerful drugs designed to destroy cancer cells or to interfere with their development. The main objective of chemotherapy is to achieve remission. In remission, there are no longer any symptoms of the

How Does Chemo Work?

Chemo drugs are poisons that kill cells. They target cells that are actively dividing. Cancer cells divide much more often than most normal body cells. Some healthy cells do divide actively, though. These include cells in bone marrow, hair, skin, and the lining of the mouth and digestive system. Chemo drugs can't tell the difference between cancer cells and normal cells, so they can damage some normal cells, too. This causes unpleasant side effects such as hair loss, nausea and vomiting, numbness and tingling of the fingers and toes, mouth sores, headache, fatigue, and loss of appetite. The side effects usually are not life-threatening and go away after the treatment is completed.

disease. Laboratory tests show that the tumor has not grown back. That does not mean that the disease is cured, however. Cancer cells may still be present in small numbers somewhere in the body, and they may return sometime in the future. The return of a patient's cancer is called a recurrence. However a person can stay in remission for months or many years. A recurrence is most likely to develop within five years after treatment is completed. After five years, a recurrence is unlikely, and the disease is considered "cured."

Chemotherapy weakens the immune system (the body's defenses). Chemo drugs can kill disease-fighting white blood cells, which divide actively. So patients may get sick easily during treatment. They may have trouble fighting off even a simple cold. A cold could lead to more serious infections, which could become life-threatening. Therefore, patients need to take extra precautions against exposure to germs during treatment.

Radiation Therapy

Radiation therapy involves the use of high doses of X-rays to kill or damage cancer cells deep inside the body. A special machine is used to direct an X-ray beam to the area of the body that needs treatment. Cancer

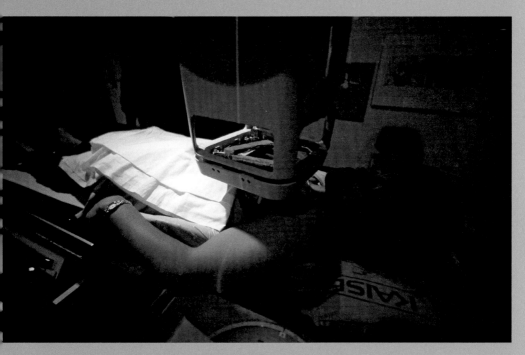

A technician accompanies a patient about to undergo radiation therapy. An X-ray beam will kill or damage cells in a specific area of the body that needs treatment.

cells are destroyed because the X-rays damage their ability to divide. As in chemotherapy, some normal cells are also killed in radiation therapy. However, in radiation therapy, the healthy areas can be shielded from the radiation exposure to protect as many normal cells as possible. The treatment is done every weekday for more than five to six weeks.

Radiation therapy does have some possible dangers. Some people experience mild burns, scarring, nausea, vomiting, and weight loss. Symptoms usually go away within a month or two after treatment. In rare cases, however, there may be a longer-term danger: Radiation therapy can actually *cause* cancer by producing mutations in the cells' DNA.

Radiation therapy is often used in combination with surgery or chemotherapy. It may be used to reduce the size of the tumor before surgery, to destroy remaining cancer cells after surgery, or in some cases as the main treatment.

Hormone Therapy

Women who test positive for the hormone receptor may be treated with hormone therapy. In these women, estrogen hormones help cancer cells grow and multiply when they attach to special proteins on their surface, called hormone receptors. The idea behind hormone therapy is to keep the hormones from getting to any cancer cells that may be left after surgery. To prevent a recurrence, many patients have hormone therapy after they finish chemotherapy.

The most common type of hormone therapy involves using drugs such as tamoxifen. Tamoxifen works by attaching to the cancer cell's hormone receptor so that the hormone cannot get to it. Some other drugs, called aromatase inhibitors, work by lowering the estrogen level in the body so that the cancer cells cannot get enough of the hormone to grow. These drugs are used to treat early-stage breast cancer. They have become the standard treatment for women who develop breast cancer after menopause. The most common side effects of hormone therapy are hot flashes, blood clots in the leg veins, and an increase in the risk of uterine cancer. Aromatase inhibitors may also cause joint pain.

5

Breast Cancer Survivors

KAREN PALOTAS was never a big fan of exercise and eating healthy foods. At age fifty-four, she weighed nearly two hundred pounds (about 90 kilograms). The most exercise she got, Karen admits, was walking from the kitchen to the couch carrying a bag of chips or some other kind of junk food. All that changed in December 2000 when she was diagnosed with breast cancer.

After Karen was diagnosed, she got a double mastectomy. She then received six months of chemotherapy and about seven weeks of radiation. She was a breast cancer survivor. Karen decided to make some big changes in her life. Her main focus now was her health. She started a new career as an owner of a

Karen Palotas began to exercise and eat healthier food after her breast cancer diagnosis in 2000.

fitness center. "You have to care about your health when you're done with your treatment," Karen said. "You change things you're doing wrong, and you look at it as a second shot at life. The day comes when you decide you want to live and grow old with your husband. To do that, you have to be willing to pick up where the doctors left off."[1]

Karen dedicated her life to getting physically fit. She started a rigorous exercise program and ate healthy foods, which included lots of fresh fruits and vegetables. Eventually, she lost 70 pounds (32 kg) and went from a size 22 to a size 8. "I wasn't this healthy when I was twenty," Karen says.[2]

Stay Strong and Healthy

Living with cancer is not all about sickness and cancer treatments. It's about staying healthy. In order to do that, cancer patients need to exercise, get enough sleep, and eat the right foods. All these things help to boost the body's immune system, and when the immune system is strong, the patient can fight the cancer more effectively. A strong body can also help a person handle cancer treatments better, as well as the side effects.

During cancer treatment, the patient may feel sick and tired and is probably not in the mood to do much of anything. However, resting too much can weaken muscles, and the body's circulation gets less effective, too. When they're feeling up to it, cancer patients should try to exercise. Physical activity is very important in strengthening the muscles, heart, lungs, and overall circulation. Furthermore, it keeps the whole body strong.

Exercise is also a good way to stay at a healthy

weight. As was mentioned earlier, obesity can increase the risk of breast cancer or a recurrence. (Remember, fat tissue produces estrogen, which feeds cancer cells.) People don't need to run two miles a day to get physically fit. Exercise can be gardening, taking long walks, or doing housework—anything that moves the body. A number of studies have shown that women who exercise an hour or more a week after breast cancer treatment have a better survival rate than those who do not exercise at all.

Exercise is good not only for the body but for the mind as well. When the body is active, chemicals called endorphins work in the brain to produce happy feelings. Exercise can also make people feel good about themselves, giving them a sense of accomplishment and independence.

Getting enough sleep is just as important as getting enough exercise. During the day people use a lot of energy, especially during cancer treatments. Sleep gives the body a chance to rest. While a person is asleep, the body can heal cuts, bruises, and sore muscles. A lack of sleep weakens the body's defenses, which makes it harder to fight off disease germs.

Cancer patients need to watch what they eat as well.

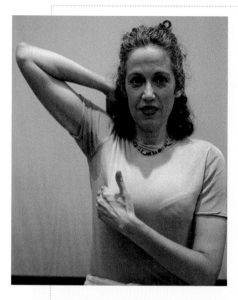

Doctor Uses Yoga to Teach About Breast Self-Exams

Dr. Ruth Lerman is a two-time breast cancer survivor. After the second time, she wanted to find some kind of activity that would help in her recovery, in addition to the surgery, chemotherapy, and radiation treatments she was already receiving. "I wanted to regain a sense of wholeness and peace," she said. She started to practice yoga. It helped her relax and relieve her stress.

Meanwhile, Dr. Lerman found that her whole life was changing. She had been a doctor specializing in geriatrics, the treatment of elderly people. Now, however, her interests were focused on breast cancer. She took a job at the Beaumont Breast Care Center in Michigan and trained with the surgeons and radiologists there. She also began training as a yoga instructor.

A balanced diet that includes a variety of healthy foods will help to strengthen the immune system. It should be high in complex carbohydrates and low in fat, with plenty of protein. Complex carbohydrates help to boost the body's energy level. They may include grains (cereals, pastas, rice, flour, and bran), legumes (beans,

Later she combined these two fields. She started a yoga workshop in which she also taught the women how to do breast self-exams. She had been concerned that many women do not do BSEs because they are too busy, too afraid of finding a suspicious lump, or simply do not know how. The relaxing atmosphere of a yoga class, with dim lights in a quiet room, seemed perfect for teaching women the BSE techniques.

Dr. Lerman leads two support groups for women with breast cancer. She helps them to understand what the diagnosis and treatment will mean in their lives and to cope with the emotional problems that may develop. Dr. Lerman wears street clothes at work, rather than a doctor's white coat, to help her patients feel more comfortable with her.

Dr. Lerman's patients have had a very positive response to her programs. "I'm convinced that teaching women about their own breasts in a relaxed, supportive atmosphere is better," she notes. "I use my own experience, openness, and vulnerability [along] with yoga to help women relax, focus, and learn."[3]

lentils, and peas), potatoes, and other vegetables. Some studies have indicated a possible link between fat and cancer, including breast cancer. So doctors recommend that a healthy diet should contain less than 20 to 30 percent fat. Protein is very important because it is needed to build, maintain, and repair cells. During cancer treatment, the body needs enough protein to repair damaged tissues and help to keep the immune system strong.

Dieters typically count the calories in the foods they eat to make sure they don't eat too much. Cancer patients, however, need to count calories to make sure they are eating enough to support their body's needs. Many cancer patients tend to lose weight. They don't just lose stored body fat, they also lose muscle and become weak and tired. Weight loss may become especially severe in the late stages of cancer. This weight loss is partly due to reduced appetite, but changes in the way the body uses food may also play a role. An actively growing tumor uses far more than its share of calories, starving the normal cells. Meanwhile, the body needs extra nutrients to recover after surgery and other treatments.

A healthy diet should also include vitamins and minerals, which are essential for keeping the body systems working properly. Research studies suggest that certain vitamins might help prevent cancer. These are vitamins A, C, and E. They help protect DNA from mutations that may lead to cancer.

Certain foods also contain cancer-fighting

Fight Cancer with Food[4]

Here are some of the best foods for fighting cancer:

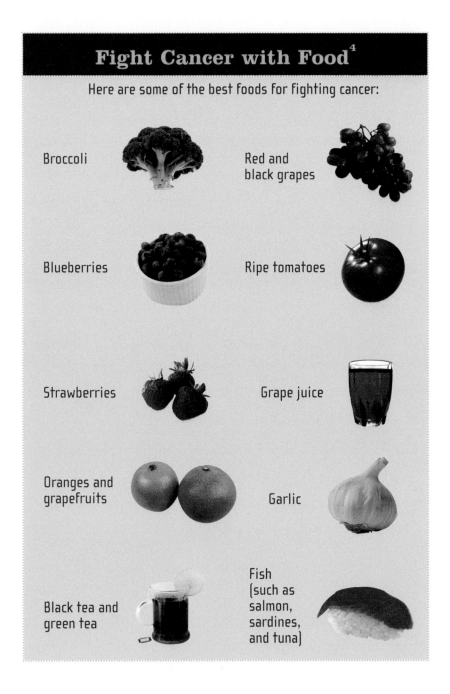

Broccoli

Red and
black grapes

Blueberries

Ripe tomatoes

Strawberries

Grape juice

Oranges and
grapefruits

Garlic

Black tea and
green tea

Fish
(such as
salmon,
sardines,
and tuna)

chemicals. Fish oil, for example, contains omega-3 fatty acids that can help keep cancer genes under control. "Eat your fruits and veggies" is good advice, too, especially if they are brightly colored. Researchers have discovered that various plant products contain unique phytochemicals (complex chemicals found only in plants) that lower the risk of developing cancer. Some of the cancer-fighting phytochemicals are now available as supplements, but doctors say that the foods in a varied diet are the best way to get them.

Getting Support

Cancer patients are able to cope much better when they have a good support system of understanding people. Supportive family and friends who stick by the patients no matter what will help them through their battle. However, not all relationships can withstand the stresses involved in battling a disease. For example, sometimes the difficulties can put a serious strain on a marriage.

Support groups can be very helpful for people with cancer. These groups are made up of people who are currently coping with cancer or are cancer survivors. Being able to talk about symptoms, fears, and treatment decisions with people who *really* understand can be a big help emotionally for someone who has recently been diagnosed or is struggling with side effects or setbacks during treatment. Some support groups actually meet in person, but telephone and Internet support groups are also available. In some cases, support groups include only present and former cancer patients. There are also more formally organized groups that are led by a therapist or other health-care professional who can provide guidance in coping. The American Cancer Society and other organizations listed at the end of this book sponsor support groups or can provide information about contacting them.

6

Preventing Breast Cancer

OR NEARLY THIRTY YEARS, Angela T. (not her real name) felt like a ticking time bomb. Breast cancer ran in her family. Her mother and her mother's three sisters all had had breast cancer by the time they were forty-five years old. She also had two cousins who had been diagnosed with breast cancer in their thirties. Ever since high school, when Angela found out about her family history of breast cancer, she had been concerned about her own body and health. She worried all the time about when breast cancer was going to finally strike her.

Angela spent much of her adult life going to doctors on a regular basis. She was frequently checking her breasts and finding strange-looking lumps or unusually dense tissue she wanted to get checked out. She went through years of testing—breast exams, mammograms, sonograms, MRIs, and biopsies—and no sign of cancer. Even so, Angela was sure her time was coming.

At forty-nine years old, Angela joined a genetic-testing program at Memorial Sloan-Kettering Cancer Center, so that she could be tested for the BRCA gene mutation. She knew that with her family history, it was likely that she carried the mutated breast cancer gene. Before getting tested, however, Angela first had to get genetic counseling. The sessions helped her think about what she would do if she got a positive result. Often she had to deal with her friends' constantly asking her, "Why do you want to know?" But Angela could not handle the not-knowing and the worry of waiting for it to happen.

Angela finally took the blood test about a year after her first genetic-counseling session. Several weeks later, she was told that she tested positive for the BRCA mutation. Angela had already had time to think about what she was going to do if the test was positive. She decided to have a preventive double mastectomy. This seemed rather extreme to her friends, and even to a number of doctors she had seen. To Angela, the decision made sense. She had spent too many years watching her loved ones get sick and finally get better, only to have the cancer return two or three years later. And then she had to watch them die. She didn't want that to happen to her, even if it meant removing both of her breasts. Angela needed to find a doctor who could see her point of view and do the surgery. Finally she found a doctor who agreed to do the procedure. Angela's husband and children supported her decision. She went through with the mastectomy, and later had breast implants put in. Angela does not have any regrets about her decision.[1]

Testing for BRCA Mutations

With just a simple blood test, a woman can find out if her family history of breast cancer is caused by a BRCA1 or BRCA2 mutation. Some people wonder how this kind of knowledge can really help. If a woman finds out she is carrying a BRCA mutation, she may become worried all the time. She may live her life in fear, just waiting to get breast cancer. Actually, the purpose of genetic testing is to allow a person to take steps to try to prevent the disease, or to detect it early when it is most treatable.

Usually it is recommended that family members who have had breast cancer be tested for the BRCA mutation. If the test is positive, identifying the gene mutation (BRCA1 or BRCA2) could make it easier for doctors to look for it in other family members.

Anyone who is thinking about genetic testing should seek genetic counseling to go over all the options. People need to remember that testing positive for the BRCA mutation does not mean that they will get breast cancer, but it greatly increases the risk. (Remember, up to 85 percent of people with the mutation will develop breast cancer.) There are many other things to consider. How would a person handle a positive test result? What are her plans? Knowing about this mutation could help women get tested more regularly. However, there are also some other options that may greatly reduce their risk or actually prevent them from developing breast cancer.

Preventive Mastectomy

Some women who test positive for the BRCA mutation, such as Angela, may choose a rather extreme method of prevention—getting a double mastectomy. Many people have trouble understanding why someone would want to have a mastectomy when they do not have cancer and may never get cancer. However, people like

Treatment from a Tree

Tamoxifen was first discovered in 1962, when researchers were testing the use of various plant chemicals as drugs to stop cancer cells. Tamoxifen was found in the bark of the Pacific yew, an evergreen tree that grows in the rainforests of the Pacific Northwest. This tree grows very

slowly; it normally takes four hundred years to grow a Pacific yew that would provide enough tamoxifen to treat just a single breast cancer patient. At first, researchers worried that the tree would become extinct if the new drug became widely used. Soon, however, it was discovered that Pacific yews grow much faster if they are planted in open farmland, where they get much more sunlight than they do in their native forests. Then scientists learned how to make the drug in the laboratory, so the trees no longer had to be used.

Tamoxifen has some unpleasant side effects, such as hot flashes, joint pains, and ankle swelling. Scientists are developing new drugs that work just as well on breast cancer cells but are less harmful to the body. In 2006, cancer researchers reported that one of these newer drugs, raloxifene (Evista), is just as effective as tamoxifen, with fewer side effects.

Angela see things differently. They see the operation as a way to take control and stop living in fear. It can bring them peace of mind.

Preventive mastectomy is controversial, and some doctors are not willing to perform it on healthy people. Women considering this surgery need to think carefully before making a decision. They should consider their emotional reactions, the financial costs, and possible risks of the operation compared to the benefits of possibly preventing breast cancer.

Targeting Hormones

Another option for women with a high risk for breast cancer is taking tamoxifen. Remember that this drug works by preventing cancer cells from picking up estrogen. It also helps reduce the risk of developing breast cancer. (It works only for types of breast cancer sensitive to hormones, however.)

Women who have already had children may choose to have their ovaries surgically removed. The ovaries make most of the body's estrogen. With the estrogen level greatly reduced, the risk of breast cancer is lowered.

7

Breast Cancer and the Future

RIBBONS HAVE BECOME symbols to Americans. Different colors represent different causes. The practice caught on in 1979, when Penne Laingen's husband was taken hostage in Iran. She told reporters that she had tied yellow ribbons around the trees in her front yard—inspired by the 1973 hit song "Tie a Yellow Ribbon 'Round the Old Oak Tree"— in hopes that her husband would come home again. All across the nation, Americans showed their support by displaying yellow ribbons.

The yellow ribbons came out again in 1990 in support of the American troops fighting in the Persian Gulf War. Around the same time, AIDS activists felt that they needed a ribbon to support those who had died from the devastating disease. They chose a bright red for their ribbon. Then in early 1992, newspaper columnist Liz Smith wrote about Charlotte Haley, a sixty-eight-year-old woman who created her own peach-colored ribbons for breast cancer. Her grandmother, sister, and daughter had all had breast cancer. Charlotte included a card with each ribbon that read: *The National Cancer Institute annual budget is $1.8 billion, only 5 percent goes for cancer prevention. Help us wake up our legislators and America by wearing this ribbon.* She handed out cards to people in supermarkets and also sent them to popular columnists such as Dear Abby and other well-known women, including former First Ladies.

Around the same time, Alexandra Penney, then the editor of *Self* magazine, was hoping to create a breast cancer ribbon for the magazine's Breast Cancer Awareness Month issue. She read about Charlotte Haley's peach ribbons and contacted her. Alexandra told Charlotte that if they combined their efforts, her peach ribbon for breast cancer awareness would get national attention. Charlotte refused, saying that the magazine was too commercial.

Alexandra still wanted to go ahead with the ribbons.

Race for the Cure

Thousands of participants in cities across the country walk or run in the Susan G. Komen Breast Cancer Foundation's annual Race for the Cure, which raises money for breast cancer awareness and research. These two photos were taken in Washington, D.C.

The lawyers working for the magazine suggested that she change the color of the ribbon. The new color, they decided, would be pink, a color that could represent all women. In fall 1992, Estée Lauder makeup counters handed out 1.5 million ribbons, along with a card that described how to do a proper breast self-exam. They also collected over 200,000 signatures on letters asking the White House to increase the money for breast cancer research.

A year later, the pink ribbon had become a national symbol for breast cancer. More and more companies

Stamping Out Breast Cancer

In 1998, the U.S. Postal Service offered the Breast Cancer Research Stamp—the first postage stamp in history to raise money for a specific cause. Each stamp cost a little more than regular stamps, and the profits went toward breast cancer research. By November 2005, more than 657 million Breast Cancer Research Stamps had been sold, and nearly $50 million had been raised for breast cancer research.[2]

First Lady Hillary Rodham Clinton officially issued the breast cancer research postage stamp in 1998. Seventy percent of the net proceeds is donated to breast cancer research.

joined the fight against breast cancer, helping to raise millions of dollars. Between 1991 and 1996, federal funding for breast cancer increased sharply, from $90 million a year to over $550 million. In addition, the American Cancer Society found that the number of women who were getting yearly mammograms and clinical breast exams had more than doubled during the 1990s.[1]

Pink ribbons are still a symbol for breast cancer awareness. Raising awareness has been an important focus for breast cancer organizations. Many women are now getting diagnosed earlier and therefore have a better chance for survival. Another important result has been raising more money for developing better tests and treatments.

Drugs on Target

One of the most promising areas of cancer research today is the development of drugs designed to kill cells of a particular kind of cancer. They work by zeroing in on the target—the cancer—and killing *only* cancer cells, not normal cells. Other cancer treatments, such as chemotherapy and radiation, kill both cancer cells and healthy cells, which results in terrible side effects.

Since healthy cells remain unharmed when targeted drugs are used, there are fewer side effects. Many scientists are calling these

> One of the most promising areas of cancer research today is the development of drugs designed to kill cells of a particular kind of cancer.

targeted drugs the "wave of the future."

Researchers have already identified a number of genes linked with the development of breast cancer. The BRCA1 and BRCA2 genes were discussed earlier. In addition, it has been found that 25 to 30 percent of breast cancer patients have extra copies of a gene called HER2, which makes cells sensitive to human growth factor, a hormone controlling growth.[3] The extra copies of the gene result in uncontrolled cell growth—cancer. Identifying cancer genes gives researchers a way of making drugs that target these specific genes. A drug called Herceptin has already been developed to block the effects of the HER2 gene. It targets only cells with extra copies of the gene, leaving healthy cells alone. This way it can stop tumor growth without producing the typical side effects of chemotherapy drugs. Doctors can now test for HER2 genes and thus find out exactly which patients will get the best results from the drug.

In 1998 the Food and Drug Administration (FDA)

approved Herceptin for treating patients with advanced breast cancer. Even after the cancer has metastasized, patients who received Herceptin along with chemotherapy survived up to one third longer than those who had only chemotherapy.[4] More recent studies show that patients in the early stages of breast cancer can also be helped. Test results on about 6,500 women with early breast cancer, reported in 2005, revealed that Herceptin cuts the risk of recurrence by 50 percent.[5]

Herceptin is injected directly into the blood. A newer drug, Tykerb, also targets the HER2 gene but can be taken in pill form. This drug can pass from the bloodstream into the brain. According to early studies, when Tykerb is given with chemotherapy, the cancer is less likely to spread to the brain.[6]

Meanwhile, several groups of researchers are working on vaccines that can make the patient's own white blood cells attack and kill breast cancer cells. One experimental vaccine uses the protein made by the HER2 gene to train a special kind of white blood cells called killer T cells. Another uses the gene for a protein called mammoglobin, which is found in 80 percent of breast cancers. Both vaccines have worked on experimental mice, making their breast cancer tumors melt away. The next step will be clinical trials on human patients.[7]

High-Tech Tests

Mammography has been the standard screening test for breast cancer since the 1960s. Mammograms have saved lives by helping to detect cancers earlier, while they are more easily treated. However, mammograms can miss very early breast cancers—those too small to detect or hidden by dense breast tissue. They also give a number of "false positives"—findings that look like cancer but turn out to be benign. Women who receive such results need to have extra tests or even surgery. Doctors would like to have better ways of testing. They want to be able to detect breast cancer even earlier and spare women worry and expense by reducing false positive results.

Computers are now playing a big role in the development of new mammography techniques. In *digital mammography*, a computer turns the X-ray picture into a digital image instead of recording it on X-ray film. Changing the magnification, brightness, or contrast of the digital image brings out details that would not be noticed on an X-ray film. This is especially helpful in finding tumors in younger women with dense breast tissue. Digital images can be stored much more easily than films, and they can be sent electronically to other locations to be viewed by other experts. A further advance is *computer-aided detection and diagnosis* (CAD). A computer program is used to point out suspicious areas to be checked more closely by a radiologist.

Another imaging technique sometimes used for detecting cancer is *thermography*. An infrared camera takes pictures of the heat radiation given off by the breasts. Cancerous tumors tend to be warmer than nearby normal tissues, so they stand out as bright spots on the images.

Most experts believe that mammography is as good or better than thermography for breast cancer screening. Thermography does have some advantages, however. No radiation at all is sent into the body—not even heat, which is produced by the body itself. The breasts do not have to be flattened, as they are during a mammogram. Thermograms do not detect microcalcifications, though, and do not give as much detail as mammograms do. Some experts believe that thermograms can detect cancer much earlier, before a tumor grows large enough to be seen on a mammogram.

This view is still very controversial. In 2006, clinical trials were under way at five hospitals in the United States to find out how useful computerized thermal imaging may be in detecting breast cancer.[8]

Molecular breast imaging, developed at the Mayo Clinic, uses a specially designed "gamma camera." It takes pictures of tiny tumors that are too small to be detected by a mammogram. Women with suspicious findings on mammograms are injected with tiny amounts of a radioactive chemical, too small to cause any harm. The radioactive chemical gives off gamma rays and tends to build up in cells that are very active—such as cancer cells. The researchers say their technique is much better than mammography in detecting cancer in women with dense breast tissue.[9]

* * *

There have been many amazing advances in cancer research since the 1970s. New types of drugs are already helping many people with cancer to live longer than before. High-tech diagnostic testing, which makes it possible to detect breast cancer in the early stages, also increases the chances for successful treatment.

In the mid-1970s, about 75 percent of women diagnosed with breast cancer survived for at least five years after treatment. By 2006, the five-year survival rate was 90 percent. When breast cancer is diagnosed early, before it spreads to the lymph nodes, the survival rate is nearly 98 percent.[10] There are about 2.3 million breast cancer *survivors* in the United States today.[11]

Questions and Answers

I just found out my mom has breast cancer. Does that mean that she's going to die? These days, more and more people are surviving breast cancer. If your mom's cancer was found early, she has a better than 90 percent chance of surviving. If the cancer has spread to other parts of the body, the condition is much more serious, but there are still treatments that may help.

The chemotherapy treatments are making my mom really sick and miserable. How is it helping her get better? The drugs are killing the cancer cells, but they are also harming some healthy body cells that normally divide actively, such as those in the hair follicles and in the lining of the stomach and intestines. Your mom will feel better once the cancer cells have been wiped out and the treatments can be stopped.

Both my mom and my grandmother had breast cancer. Does that mean that I'll get it, too? Not necessarily. The genes you inherit can increase your risk of getting cancer, but your lifestyle and environment also play important roles. Even if you have inherited genes linked with breast cancer, you may never get the disease. If you have an increased risk, however, it is important to do monthly breast self-exams and have regular checkups. Then if breast cancer does develop, it is more likely to be detected at an early, treatable stage.

Are people with bigger breasts more likely to get breast cancer? No. The size of breasts have nothing to do with whether or not a person will get breast cancer. Everybody has breast tissue. Even men can get breast cancer (although it is very rare). However, women with larger breasts may have a harder time trying to feel for a lump.

Do breast implants cause breast cancer? No, but they may make it more difficult to find a lump. When getting a mammogram, women with implants should tell the technician about them. The technician will need to take extra pictures to get different views.

At what age should girls start doing breast self-exams? Even though most breast cancer cases are found in women over forty, it is best to start doing breast self-exams at around twenty years old. This way, a woman can become familiar with her breasts, in the way they look and feel. Then as she gets older, she will notice when something doesn't feel right, such as finding an unusual lump.

What's the big deal about a girl starting puberty early, like nine years old? What does that have to do with breast cancer? When a girl starts puberty, her body releases a lot of hormones, including estrogen, which has been linked to breast cancer. Scientists have found that estrogen feeds cancer cells, helping them to grow and multiply. The more exposure a woman has to estrogen during her lifetime, the greater her chances of developing breast cancer. So the risk is increased the earlier she starts puberty and the later she starts menopause (the time at which a woman stops getting her monthly period).

Breast Cancer Timeline

1600 B.C. Egyptians record earliest descriptions of breast cancer in the Ebers Papyrus.

400 B.C. Greek physician Hippocrates uses the term *cancer* to describe a group of diseases involving tumors, lumps, and bumps.

A.D. 100s Greek physician Leonides performs the first recorded surgical removal of the breast (mastectomy).

A.D. 200 Greek physician Galen believes that cancer is caused by too much bile in the blood and recommends treatments involving special diets, bloodletting, and herbal mixtures placed on the diseased breast.

1700 French physician Claude Gendron publishes a book explaining that cancers are solid structures that form from body tissues such as nerves, glands, or lymphatic vessels.

1757 French surgeon Henri Le Dran says that cancer is a local disease that first spreads to the lymph nodes, then to the lymphatic system, and from there to other parts of the body.

Mid-1800s German physician Johannes Müller reports that cancerous tumors are made up of abnormal cells that look different from normal cells under a microscope.

1867 British surgeon Charles Moore introduces the radical mastectomy, a procedure that removes the breast, chest muscle, and lymph nodes.

1894 American surgeon William Halsted publishes a report that helps to make the radical mastectomy standard treatment for breast cancer.

1895 German physicist Wilhelm Conrad Roentgen discovers X-rays.

1896 Emile Grubbe becomes the first person to use X-rays to treat breast cancer.

Early 1900s Paul Ehrlich coins the term *chemotherapy*.

1906 British surgeon W. Sampson Handley becomes the first to use radiation therapy.

1913 German surgeon Albert Salomon runs X-ray studies of breast tissue from 3,000 mastectomies. His results form the basis for mammography.

1922	Geoffrey Keynes introduces lumpectomy plus radiation as a breast cancer treatment.
1930s	Mammography begins to be used for diagnosis of breast cancer.
1946	Nitrogen mustard is used for cancer chemotherapy.
1960s	Mammograms have proven to be an effective diagnostic tool.
1969	The first X-ray machines used only for mammography are introduced.
1975	Studies led by Bernard Fisher show that a radical mastectomy is unnecessary, and a modified radical mastectomy becomes the preferred treatment for breast cancer.
1985	Researchers identify the HER2 gene as linked to cancer.
1990	The National Cancer Institute declares lumpectomy plus radiation as the preferred treatment for early-stage breast cancer. Researchers identify BRCA1 as the first gene linked to breast cancer.
Early 1990s	A pink ribbon becomes a symbol of breast cancer awareness.

1998 .... Tamoxifen is the first drug used in the prevention of breast cancer.

FDA approves Herceptin, which targets the HER2 gene, for the treatment of advanced breast cancer.

2005 .... The BRCA2 gene is found in other types of cancer in addition to breast cancer.

Clinical trials show that Herceptin prevents recurrence in 50 percent of women with early-stage breast cancer.

2006 .... Clinical trials show that raloxifene (Evista) is as effective as tamoxifen in preventing breast cancer, with fewer side effects.

For More Information

American Cancer Society
1599 Clifton Road, NE
Atlanta, GA 30329
Toll-Free: 800-ACS-2345
Phone: 404-320-3333
Website: http://www.cancer.org

American Institute for Cancer Research (AICR)
1759 R Street NW
Washington, DC 20009
Toll-free: 800-843-8114
Phone: 202-328-7744
E-mail: aicrweb@aicr.org
Website: http://www.aicr.org

Breastcancer.org
111 Forest Avenue 1R
Narberth, PA 19072
Website: http://www.breastcancer.org

Cancer Care
National Office
275 Seventh Avenue, Floor 22
New York, NY, 10001
Telephone support groups: 800-813-HOPE (4673)
E-mail: info@cancercare.org
Website: http://www.cancercare.org

Centers for Disease Control and Prevention
National Center for Chronic Disease Prevention and
Health Promotion
Division of Cancer Prevention and Control
Mail Stop K-64, 4770 Buford Highway, NE
Atlanta, GA 30341-3717
Toll-free: 800-CDC-INFO (800-232-4636)
Fax: 770-488-4760
E-mail: cdcinfo@cdc.gov
Website: http://www.cdc.gov/cancer

The National Breast Cancer Coalition
1101 17th Street, NW, Suite 1300
Washington, D.C. 20036
Toll-free: 800-622-2838
Phone: 202-296-7477
Fax: 202-265-6854
Website: http://www.natlbcc.org/

National Breast Cancer Foundation, Inc.
2600 Network Boulevard
Suite 300
Frisco, TX 75034
E-mail: info@nationalbreastcancer.org
Website: http://www.nationalbreastcancer.org

National Cancer Institute
NCI Public Inquiries Office
6116 Executive Boulevard
Room 3036A
Bethesda, MD 20892-8322
Toll-free: 800-4-CANCER (800-422-6237)
Website: http://cancer.gov

The Susan G. Komen Breast Cancer Foundation
5005 LBJ Freeway, Suite 250
Dallas, TX 75244
Phone: 972-855-1600
Fax: 972-855-1605
Helpline: 800-462-9273
Website: http://www.komen.org/

Y-ME National Breast Cancer Organization
212 W. Van Buren, Suite 1000
Chicago, IL 60607-3903
Phone: 312-986-8338
Phone support: 800-221-2141
Website: http://www.y-me.org/

Chapter Notes

Chapter 1. Cells Gone Wild

1. Stone Phillips, "Melissa's Brave Comeback," MSNBC.com, February 22, 2005, <http://www.msnbc.msn.com/id/6994469/> (April 28, 2006).

2. Stone Phillips, "Melissa Etheridge's Anthem of Hope," MSNBC.com, October 16, 2005, <http://www.msnbc.msn.com/id/9673481/> (April 28, 2006).

Chapter 2. Breast Cancer Through the Ages

1. "New Attitudes Ushered In by Betty Ford," *New York Times,* October 17, 1987, p. 9.

2. Zenon Rayter, ed., "History of Breast Cancer Therapy," Cambridge University Press, January 2003, <http://assets.cambridge.org/052149/6322/excerpt/052 1496322_excerpt. pdf> (May 25, 2006).

3. Richard A. Evans, *Understanding Cancer: The Cancer Breakthrough You've Never Heard Of,* Texas Cancer Center, 2001, excerpt found on website: <http://www.texascancercenter.com/cancerhistory. html> (May 22, 2006).

4. The National Surgical Adjuvant Breast and Bowel Project (NSABP), "An Historical Overview," April 6, 2006, <http://foundation.nsabp.org/Media/ about_nsabp.htm> (November 4, 2006).

5. Ibid.

Chapter 3. What Is Breast Cancer?

1. Cynthia Wang, "Rebuilding a Body, Restoring a Soul," *People Magazine,* October 24, 2005, pp. 103-104.

2. Jennifer O'Neill, Melanie Bromley, et al., "A Survivor Battles Breast Cancer," *US Weekly,* October 24, 2005, pp. 64-65.

3. Dr. Ken Lichtenfeld, American Cancer Society, "Breast Cancer Today," *The National Women's Health Information Center's Featured Health Articles,* October 2006, <http://www.4woman.gov/editor/oct06/> (November 5, 2006); American Cancer Society, "What Are the Key Statistics for Breast Cancer?" revised September 18, 2006, <http://www.cancer.org/docroot/CRI/content/CRI_2_4_1X_What_are_the_Key_statistics_for_breast_cancer_5.asp> (November 4, 2006).

4. American Cancer Society, "Breast Cancer Facts &Figures20052006," 2005, <http://www.cancer.org/downloads/STT/CAFF2005BrF.pdf> (May 10, 2006).

5. Susan G. Komen Breast Cancer Foundation, "MaleBreastCancer," 2006, <http://www.komen.org/intradoccgi/idc_cgi_isapi.dll?IdcService=SS_GET_PAGE&ssDocName=s_002755> (December 24, 2006).

6. American Cancer Society, "Breast Cancer Facts & Figures 2005-2006."

7. "What is Breast Cancer?" AstraZeneca Pharmaceuticals, ©2006, <http://www.getbcfacts.com/about/whatis.asp> (May 25, 2006).

8. Breastcancer.org, "Cancer Risk and Abnormal Breast Cancer Genes," modified May 19, 2004

<http://www.breastcancer.org/genetics_cancer_risk.html>
(June 6, 2006).

Chapter 4. Diagnosis and Treatment

1. Alex Tresniowski and Laura Figueroa, "For the Love of Mom," *People Magazine,* March 27, 2006, pp. 163-164.

2. Erin Sullivan, "Dakoda Dowd, 13, Fulfills Her Mother's Dream," *The Mercury News,* April 27, 2006 <http://www.mercurynews.com/mld/mercurynews/sports/14444394.htm> (May 1, 2006).

3. "Mammograms and Other Breast Imaging Procedures," American Cancer Society, revised September 26, 2006, <http://www.cancer.org/docroot/CRI/content/CRI_2_6x_Mammography_and_other_Breast_Imaging_Procedures_5.asp> (November 3, 2006).

Chapter 5. Breast Cancer Survivors

1. Meg Nugent, "Recovery in Motion," *The Star-Ledger,* Newark, NJ, October 31, 2005, pp. 25, 32.

2. Ibid.

3. Patricia Anstett, "Yoga Makes Breast Self-Exams Easier, Doctor Says," *Pioneer News,* October 17, 2002, p. 8, <http://pioneer.csueastbay.edu/PioneerWeb/PioneerNews10-17-02/PioneerNews10-17-02-Page8.pdf> (June 19, 2006).

4. "11 Cancer-Fighting Foods," Stanford Prevention Research Center, 2005, <http://lslw.stanford.edu/11Foods.html> (November 2, 2006); Neal D. Barnard, MD, "Healthy Eating for Life: Food Choices for Cancer

Prevention and Survival," The Cancer Project, 2004, <http://www.cancerproject.org/resources/pdfs/Healthy EatingforLife.pdf> (November 2, 2006); "Cancer Fighting Foods and Spices," The Cancer Cure Foundation, 2000, <http://www.cancure.org/cancer _fighting_foods.htm> (November 2, 2006).

Chapter 6. Preventing Breast Cancer

1. Craig Horowitz, "The Time-Bomb Genes," *New York Magazine*, February 8, 1999, pp. 29-33, 89.

Chapter 7. Breast Cancer and the Future

1. Sandy M. Fernandez, "Pretty in Pink," June/July 1998, <http://www.thinkbeforeyoupink.org/ Pages/PrettyInPink.html> (June 20, 2006).

2. "Breast Cancer Stamp Extended Two More Years: Almost $50 Million Raised for Breast Cancer Research So Far," Senate Committee on Homeland Security & Government Affairs, November 4, 2005, <http:// www.senate.gov/~govtaff/index.cfm?FuseAction=Press Releases.Detail&Affiliation=R&PressRelease_id=1132& Month=11&Year=2005> (June 22, 2006).

3. Dennis J. Slamon, Brian Leyland-Jones, Steven Shak, et al., "Use of Chemotherapy Plus a Monoclonal Antibody against HER2 for Metastatic Breast Cancer That Overexpresses HER2," *The New England Journal of Medicine*, March 15, 2001, p. 783, <http: //content.nejm.org/cgi/content/abstract/344/11/783> (November 4, 2006).

4. "Herceptin Transforms Survival Rates," The Royal Marsden NHS Foundation Trust, May 15, 2005,

<http://www.royalmarsden.nhs.uk/rmh/info/newsevents/pressreleases/pr15052005a> (November 4, 2006).

5. American Association for Cancer Research, "AACR Cancer Concepts: HER2," ©2006, <http://www.aacr.org/page5566.aspx> (June 20, 2006).

6. Bernardine Healy, M.D., "Closing In on a Cure," *U.S. News & World Report,* October 23, 2006, p. 67.

7. Kitta MacPherson, "Killer T-cells Melt Away Breast Cancer in Mice," [Newark, NJ] *Star-Ledger,* October 8, 2006, Section 1, pp. 1 and 14.

8. Imaginis Corporation, "Breast Cancer Diagnosis: Thermography/Computerized Thermal Imaging," July 2006,<http://imaginis.com/breasthealth/thermal_imaging.asp> (January 2, 2007).

9. "Mayo Clinic Researchers Report Success in New Molecular Breast Imaging Technique," January 11, 2005, <http://www.mayoclinic.org/news2005-rst/2571> (June 10, 2006); Beth W. Orenstein, "Think Small-Mayo Clinic Researchers Retool Scintimammography to Target Small Lesions," *Radiology Today,* Vol. 6, No. 9, p. 8, May 2, 2005, <http://www.radiologytoday.net/archive/rt_050205p8.shtml> (June 24, 2006).

10. Dr. Ken Lichtenfeld, American Cancer Society, "Breast Cancer Today," *The National Women's Health Information Center's Featured Health Articles,* October 2006, <http://www.4woman.gov/editor/oct06/> (November 5, 2006).

11. "Many Breast Cancer Survivors Neglect Mammograms," American Cancer Society, April 24, 2006, <http://www.cancer.org/docroot/NWS/content/NWS_1_1x_Many_Breast_Cancer_Survivors_Neglect_Mammograms.asp> (November 4, 2006).

Glossary

anesthetics—Drugs that temporarily numb the body and block feelings of pain.

antiseptics—Chemicals that kill disease-causing germs.

axillary nodes—Lymph nodes in the armpits.

benign—Pertaining to a noncancerous tumor.

biopsy—The removal of a small sample of tissue, cells, or fluid for microscopic examination to check for abnormalities and establish a diagnosis.

blood vessels—Tubes that carry blood to nearly all the cells of the body. They include arteries, veins, and capillaries.

BRCA gene—A *breast cancer* gene that helps in breast growth and protects against breast cancer; 85 percent of women with abnormal forms of this gene will develop breast cancer.

capillaries—Tiny, thin-walled blood vessels.

carcinogens—Cancer-causing chemicals, such as those found in cigarettes, certain foods, and industrial materials.

carcinoma—Cancers that start in epithelial tissue (covering and lining tissues). Examples include cancers of the lungs, breast, ovaries, prostate, stomach, and intestines.

cell—The basic unit of life.

chemotherapy—The use of drugs ("chemicals") to treat diseases by killing invading germs or cancerous cells or by stopping their growth and reproduction.

cyst—A fluid-filled sac. Noncancerous cysts are often found in the breast.

DNA (deoxyribonucleic acid)—The substance that carries the hereditary instructions for making proteins.

ductal carcinoma—Cancer in the ducts of the breast.

ducts—Hollow tubes that carry a fluid. Ducts in the breast carry milk.

endorphins—Chemicals released in the body that send "happy messages" to the brain.

estrogen—A female sex hormone.

fibrocystic breast changes—Lumps in the breast that may become larger and painful at certain times of the month, due to the hormonal ups and downs of the menstrual cycle.

gene—A chemical unit containing coded instructions to make a protein; genes carry hereditary traits from one generation to the next.

glands—Structures in the body that release chemicals.

glandular—Pertaining to glands.

HER2 gene—A gene that helps in growth. Extra copies of this gene are found in 25 to 30 percent of breast cancer patients.

hormones—Chemicals released into the bloodstream that help to control and regulate the body's activities.

immune system—The body's defenses against invading germs or foreign cells and tissues.

lobes—A collection of lobules.

lobules—Tiny saclike glands that produce milk during breast-feeding.

lumpectomy—A surgical procedure in which the breast tumor is removed along with some normal tissue around it. (*See* **mastectomy** and **radical mastectomy.**)

lymphatic system—A network of vessels that return filtered lymph (fluid drained from the tissues after leaking out of capillaries) to the circulatory system.

lymph nodes—Small structures scattered along the lymphatic system; they contain disease-fighting cells.

malignant—Pertaining to a cancerous tumor.

mammoglobin—A protein found in 80 percent of breast cancers.

mammogram—An X-ray of the breast.

mastectomy—A surgical procedure to remove one or both breasts to keep the cancer from spreading to other parts of the body.

menopause—A time in which a woman stops having her monthly period, and the ovaries no longer produce estrogen.

menstrual cycle—A process that prepares the female body for a possible pregnancy. It includes the production and release of hormones and the maturing and release of an ovum (egg), and thickening of the lining of the uterus. The cycle takes about a month and ends with a flow of blood as the thickened lining of the uterus breaks down.

metastasis—The spread of cancer cells to different parts of the body, where they form new tumors.

mutation—A chemical change in a gene, which may produce a new trait that can be inherited.

obesity—Extreme overweight.

ovaries—A pair of oval-shaped female sex organs in which eggs and hormones are produced.

phytochemicals—Unique chemicals found in plant food products that can promote good health.

puberty—The period of rapid growth and changes in the body as the sex organs mature and become capable of reproduction.

radiation therapy—The use of high doses of X-rays or other radiations to kill cancer cells deep inside the body.

radical mastectomy—Surgical removal of the breast, together with the underlying muscles and axillary lymph nodes, to prevent spread of breast cancer to other parts of the body.

recurrence—Return of an illness.

remission—A lessening or disappearance of disease symptoms and signs.

sex hormones—Chemicals that are produced naturally by the ovaries (in females) or testes (in males) and help to control and coordinate the normal functioning of the body's cells, organs, and systems.

testicles—Male sex glands.

testosterone—Male sex hormone.

tumor—A solid mass formed from a buildup of cells.

Further Reading

Aronson, Virginia. *Everything You Need to Know About Breast Health and Cancer Detection.* New York: The Rosen Publishing Group, Inc., 2000.

Chan, David. *Breast Cancer: Real Questions, Real Answers.* New York: Marlowe & Company, 2006.

Elk, Ronit, and Monica Morrow. *Breast Cancer for Dummies.* Hoboken, N.J.: Wiley Publishing, Inc., 2003.

Peacock, Judith. *Breast Cancer.* Minneapolis, Minn.: LifeMatters, 2001.

Pirello, Christina. *Cooking the Whole Foods Way: Your Complete, Everyday Guide to Healthy Eating.* New York: HP Books, 1997.

Vogel, Carole Garbuny. *Breast Cancer: Questions and Answers for Young Women.* Brookfield, Conn.: Twenty-First Century Books, 2001.

Internet Addresses

WebMD, Inc. Breast Cancer.
<http://www.webmd.com/hw/breast_cancer/tv3617.asp>

Cancer Care.
<http://www.cancercare.org>

Index

sex hormones, 42, 43
side effects
  of chemotherapy, 71
  of hormone therapy, 75
  of radiation therapy, 73–74
Simon, Carly, 13
sleep, 79
Smith, Jaclyn, 13
Smith, Liz, 93
Somers, Suzanne, 13
sonogram, 63, 87
spread of cancer, 34, 38, 44, 55.
  See also metastasis.
Stage 0 cancer, 67
Stage II breast cancer, 11
Stage III breast cancer, 32
Stage IV cancer, 55
staging cancer 66–67
sterilization, 22
stress, 12
sunlight, **49**
support groups, 81, 84–85
support system, 84
surgery, 7, 11, 18, 19, 20, 22, 33,
  74, 80
surgical biopsy, 65
Susan G. Komen Breast
  Foundation, **94**

T

tamoxifen, 7, 34, 74, 90, 91, 109
test for HER2 genes, 97
testicles, 42
testosterone, 42
tests
  for breast cancer, 99–101
  for metastasis, 65

thermography, 100
tiredness, 54
TNM system, 67
total mastectomy, 29, **68**
tumor, 11, 18, 19, 20, 27, **36**, 37,
  60, **61**, 62, 63, 67, 69, 72, 74,
  82, 99, 107
Tykerg, 98

U

ultrasound, 32, 62, 63
ultraviolet rays, **49**, 50
uterine cancer, 75

V

vegetables, 50, 51, 81
vitamins and minerals, 82
vomiting, 71, 73

W

weakness, 54
weight loss, 54, 73, 82
white blood cells, 41, 72, 98

X

X-ray machine, 108
X-rays, 25, 28, 49, 50, 60, 63, 67,
  72, 107

Y

yoga, 80–81